Activities, Games, and Assessment for the World Language Classroom

This best-selling book is filled with fun activities you can use to engage students in learning a world language. No matter what language and grade level you teach, you will love having a wide variety of tools at your disposal, from quick warm-up exercises to longer games and group activities.

Inside, you'll find . . .

- Essential teacher tools and student organizational tools

- Strategies to promote and monitor class participation, including student self-assessments

- Strategies to promote and assess oral proficiency, such as prompts or quick chats

- Warm-up activities and 5-minute transitional activities

- Individual, pair, and group practice activities, with modification suggestions

- Games that make learning fun, with clear directions for how to do them

- Great websites and other resources to check out for more ideas

The enhanced second edition features updated activities and technology suggestions, as well as a tabbed design so it's easier to return to your favorite sections again and again.

Bonus: The book comes with more than 30 templates—charts, rubrics, and game boards that can be photo-copied from the book or downloaded as eResources from the book product page at www.routledge.com/books/details/9781138827295. You can modify and print them for classroom use.

Amy Buttner Zimmer is a Spanish teacher at North Shore Middle School in Hartland, Wisconsin. She has taught Spanish at the elementary, middle, and high school levels and is a member of the Wisconsin Association of Foreign Language Teachers.

Other Eye On Education Books Available from Routledge
(www.routledge.com/eyeoneducation)

Getting the MOST Out of Your Interactive Whiteboard: A Practical Guide
Amy Buttner

100 Games and Activities for the Introductory Foreign Language Classroom
Thierry Boucquey et al.

A Good Start: 147 Warm-Up Activities for Spanish Class
Rebekah Stathakis

Differentiated Instruction: Guide for Foreign Language Teachers
Deborah Blaz

Bringing the Standards for Foreign Language Learning to Life
Deborah Blaz

A Collection of Performance Tasks and Rubrics: Foreign Languages
Deborah Blaz

Foreign Language Teacher's Guide to Active Learning
Deborah Blaz

Teaching Foreign Languages in the Block
Deborah Blaz

What Great Teachers Do Differently, Second Edition: 17 Things That Matter Most
Todd Whitaker

Seven Simple Secrets, Second Edition: What the BEST Teachers Know and Do!
Annette Breaux and Todd Whitaker

Rigor in Your Classroom: A Toolkit for Teachers
Barbara R. Blackburn

101 "Answers" for New Teachers and Their Mentors, Second Edition: Effective Teaching Tips for Daily Classroom Use
Annette Breaux

Activities, Games, and Assessment Strategies for the World Language Classroom

Amy Buttner Zimmer

Routledge
Taylor & Francis Group

NEW YORK AND LONDON

First published 2015
by Routledge
711 Third Avenue, New York, NY 10017

and by Routledge
2 Park Square, Milton Park, Abingdon, Oxon OX14 4RN

Routledge is an imprint of the Taylor & Francis Group, an informa business

First edition (as *Activities, Games, Assessment Strategies, and Rubrics for the Foreign Language Classroom*)

© Eye On Education 2007

© 2015 Taylor & Francis

The right of Amy Buttner Zimmer to be identified as author of this work has been asserted by her in accordance with sections 77 and 78 of the Copyright, Designs and Patents Act 1988.

Library of Congress Cataloging-in-Publication Data
Buttner, Amy.
Activities, games, and assessment strategies for the world language classroom / Amy Buttner. — Second edition.
    pages cm
  1. Language and languages—Study and teaching.   2. Teaching—Aids and devices.   I. Title.
    LB1578.B89 2014
    418.0071—dc23
    2014026114

ISBN: 978-1-138-82727-1 (hbk)
ISBN: 978-1-138-82729-5 (pbk)
ISBN: 978-1-315-73867-3 (ebk)

Typeset in Helvetica Neue
by Apex CoVantage, LLC

Printed and bound in the United States of America by Sheridan Books, Inc. (a Sheridan Group Company).

Dedicated to my two sweet little boys, Garrett and Carter

Meet the Author

Amy Buttner Zimmer is currently a middle school Spanish teacher at North Shore Middle School in Hartland, Wisconsin. Ms. Buttner Zimmer has taught Spanish at the elementary, middle, and high school levels and is a member of the Wisconsin Association of Foreign Language Teachers and regular presenter at the conference. She believes in the importance of global experiences for her students and has taken high school students to Argentina and middle school students to Costa Rica. She is dedicated to continued professional development. The first edition of this book was the result of a project designed as part of her district's Teacher Academy, a program that promoted and supported professional development and research.

Also interested in technology integration in the classroom, Ms. Buttner Zimmer is a teacher technology leader in her district and has led various staff development sessions for colleagues. She has also written the book *Getting the MOST Out of Your Interactive Whiteboard: A Practical Guide*.

Contents

Contents

Contents

Acknowledgments

When I began writing this collection in November 2006, I did so with the hope of gathering my favorite activities and games in one location, so I could write lesson plans more efficiently. I have had the great fortune to have the opportunity to revise it now for its second edition. I am grateful to Bob Sickles of Eye On Education for initially believing in my work and giving me the opportunity to share it. I am also indebted to the people whose ideas and input have made this collection possible, as it is a result of what I have learned from my students, colleagues, professional conferences, research, and reflections about my teaching practices over the past 15 years.

I would also like to express my sincere gratitude to the following people:

My parents, Tom and Charlene Buttner, for teaching me the value of a good education, always believing in me and listening to countless stories about my journey as an educator

My husband, Tim Zimmer, for his understanding, encouragement, and support through both of the writing and editing processes

My cousin, friend, and fellow educator, Jamie Hoffman, for her encouragement and her thoughtful suggestions on how to improve the format of this book

Michele Schmidt, Dale Fischer, Mary Stowasser, Therese Jilek, and Glenn Schilling for their support of my continuing growth as an educator

Terry Neumann-Hayes for her insights on rubric writing and her commitment to world language education

Linda Johnsen and Susan Tawney, who reviewed early versions of the manuscript

All of my teachers who encouraged and inspired me along the way

eResources

Many of the tools in this book can be downloaded, modified, and printed for classroom use. You can access these downloads by visiting the book product page on our website: www.routledge.com/books/details/ 9781138827295. Then click on the tab that says "eResources," and select the files. They will begin downloading to your computer.

Introduction

When I wrote this book I did so with the intention of creating a collection of activities and games to use in my classroom to improve the quality of my instruction. Oftentimes during lesson planning I found myself using the same set of activities over and over because I was short on the time needed to sort through various resource books or I would simply forget about an activity I hadn't used in a while. My solution to that problem was to make a resource book that had a variety of activities for different purposes all in one place. I have included time-honored favorites, along with others that I have learned of from my former colleague Jennifer Ladd, from professional conferences, and from research. I have tried to put a different twist on their typical uses and offer ways to extend them to get more out of the activity. The chapter on oral proficiency evolved from action research I did in my classroom and is the result of my interest in getting my beginning-level middle school students to become better speakers.

At the beginning of the activities and games chapters you will find charts to help navigate the chapters and provide a brief description of the activity. Also please note that when the term *flashcards* is used it can be taken to imply standard paper flashcards or digital ones found on sites like www.quizlet.com. Additionally, when the term *whiteboard* is used, it can refer to a standard dry erase board or a whiteboard software or app available on a computer or other mobile device.

1

Classroom Organization

Essential Teacher Tools and Ways to Use Them

Flashcards

Flashcards are a useful part of a teacher's toolbox for each unit. You can use them to review culture, content, vocabulary, and key questions. Consider using a mix of more traditional flashcards with pictures and text created on paper, as well as making use of online flashcard sources. Paper flashcards are still useful, especially for station-based activities or activities that involve moving around the room. So don't throw them out just because we are in the digital age! Students still need a mix of resources to interact with.

Flashcard Sources

- Clip art

- Student drawings

- Calendar pictures

- Magazine pictures or store fliers

Digital Flashcard Sources

There are many sources for online flashcards. The two listed are tried and true sites that integrate tools or games beyond a standard flashcard. You can search for many existing flashcards made by others and copy sets to adapt them in Quizlet. With Memrise you can search for existing courses made by other users.

- www.quizlet.com: This free site includes flashcards, games, and fill-in-the-blank practice options. Audio is also integrated. Teachers can monitor student progress, record their own audio, and add pictures to the cards for a minimal yearly fee.

- www.memrise.com: Memrise allows you to create a course with different modules, which are your study topics. Users can also create Mems to help them visualize and make textual connections, hear audio, and view a leaderboard, which adds a nice element of competition for students. Memrise has many existing courses to choose from in a variety of languages. If you use Quizlet as well, or find flashcards there you like, you can easily export your list from Quizlet and copy it to Memrise. Instead of doing the standard word-by-word entry in Memrise, you can click on Advanced. When you do so, you can copy and paste the text that is ready to export from Quizlet. You can add audio right away, not at all, or wait until you have a bit more time.

Make Flashcards That Ask Students to . . .

- Identify vocabulary words from English to target language

- Identify vocabulary terms in the target language from a description or context given in the target language

- Translate sentences

- Answer questions

- Provide the question for the answer provided

- Give beginnings or ends of sentences

- Review content-based vocabulary

- Review cultural information

Ways to Use Flashcards

Application 1: Practice Key Questions

Materials: Flashcards, whiteboard, blank sheet of paper, or tablet

Show flashcards with questions and ask students to respond with an answer or show answers and ask students to provide the question. This can be done orally, with paper flashcards or with digital flashcards projected on a screen or interactive whiteboard. You can also ask students to write down the question or answer. Another option is to set up your question flashcards at stations around the room and ask students to go to each one and write down an answer to the question that is there. Make a game out of the review by using your flashcard questions with the Casino game that is described in the Games section. If you have more access to technology, students can write answers on an app like Educreations or a whiteboard app. This is nice for students who do not have clear handwriting, as they can use the typing feature. If you have an iPad or iPhone, you can use AirPlay and run the flashcards from your mobile device. This gives you the mobility to move around the room and still project the flashcards onto the screen or interactive whiteboard. Alternatively, you can have a student control the flipping of the cards while you move about the room.

Application 2: Write Sentences or Stories

Materials: Flashcards, blank sheet of paper

Give groups of students a selection of various word or picture flashcards. Ask them to find a creative way to use all of them in a sentence, write questions, make true or false statements, or write a story using the vocabulary on the cards. Have the students illustrate their sentences, questions, or story. Also try having the students write the longest logical or illogical sentence that they can that uses all the flashcards. Differentiate by allowing more advanced students to take on the story-writing task while allowing other students to write statements or questions.

Application 3: Word Brainstorm With Alphabet Letters

Materials: Alphabet flashcards, blank sheet of paper

Use alphabet flashcards to get individuals or groups to brainstorm a list of all of the words that they know that begin with that letter. Put alphabet letters in Quizlet or a similar site and have an individual, pair, or class competition. Or have them do this by going through a few stations that have different letters or give them three to four random letters. As an additional challenge, see how long of a sentence they can form where all of the words start with the same letter.

Modification: Have students try not to guess the word you put in on the definition side of the flashcard. Give 1–2 points for each unique word they come up with as compared to yours, and take away 1 point if they pick your word. See an example here: http://quizlet.com/_p7hhc.

Application 4: Combine Unrelated Ideas

Materials: Flashcards, blank sheet of paper

Give students in pairs or groups a few unrelated or seemingly unrelated flashcards and ask them to write sentences, questions, or a story that establishes a relationship among them. Ask students to provide an illustration as well. You could select a couple words from a set of flashcards (digital or otherwise) by shuffling the set to make it random if the list is not thematic. Or you can give them the set digitally on their own to access on a device and have them pick however many you want used to form a story.

Application 5: Play Games

Materials: Flashcards

Use digital or paper flashcards to play Around the World, Five, Charades, Casino, and Pictionary, and for Inside-Outside Circle activities. For descriptions of these activities, see the table of contents for their locations.

Application 6: Discuss

Materials: Flashcards

Use your flashcards for group discussion questions. If they are teacher-led discussions for whole group or guided pair discussion questions, they can be created in a digital stack of cards. If you want questions that students can hold on to and that will be used multiple times, use cardstock that you can cut down for printing multiple sets of question cards more efficiently. You can also use the questions for Inside-Outside Circle speaking activities so students have cards with the information that they should discuss.

The Prop Box

To add excitement to class skits, dialogues, charades, sing-alongs, and other impromptu situations, a prop box is a world language classroom necessity. Fill a see-through storage box with random items, including telephones, costumes, masks, crazy hats, old clothes, sunglasses, plastic instruments, and so forth.

Prop Box Sources

Rummage sales, thrift stores, and your own closet are good places to find prop box treasures. Shop after the holidays to get good sales on Halloween masks and costumes, Santa hats, and more. The Oriental Trading Company also has fun finds for low prices. See if the drama department has any props or costumes they are willing to donate. Also, check with fellow staff members or students to see if they have something they or their parents might want to get rid of. The wackier the items you find, the better!

Ways to Use Props

Use your props to stimulate oral and writing activities. Pull out some seemingly unrelated items and ask the students to perform a skit or write a story that integrates all of them. Stage a mystery by asking the students to explain why the items were found at the scene of a crime. Ask students to wear some of the items and do a short, silent skit. Ask the performers and the audience to retell the events orally or in a written form, doing their best to narrate what happened. The prop box can provide multiple options for oral and writing activities.

Whiteboards

Student whiteboards are a great addition to any world language classroom. Using whiteboards students can draw vocabulary pictures and then label them in the target language, practice spelling, ask and answer questions, translate sentences, conjugate verbs, draw scenes, and play pair and group games. Have students hold up their answers and wait for you to check them, or post/project answers for self-checking. The students like the immediate feedback you can give them, and it is a great way for you to quickly check student progress. If you have access to tablets with a whiteboard app, or whiteboard software on computers, that adds a nice way to vary how to practice as well. Offer choice to students by allowing them to use a dry-erase board, a tablet or laptop, or pencil and paper. Some apps on iPads are Educreations, Doodle Buddy, or KidsDoodle. If you use an interactive whiteboard, students should be able to have that software installed on laptops as well.

It is nice to have a student write his or her answers on the board, standard or interactive, while students are writing their answers down as well. If students have iPads they can use AirPlay to show the work directly from their iPad as well. You can then be free to check answers of other students or move about the room. You can create your questions based on student responses or have pre-made questions in flashcards, a Google Presentation, on a PowerPoint, or in any software application you have available.

Although they can be purchased ready-made from supply companies, a very economical way to get them is from a home improvements store that sells shower board. Depending on the size you are looking for, two sheets will yield about 40 individual boards. Consider getting a variety of sizes, some smaller for individual practice and others larger for group use.

Ways to Use Whiteboards

Note: In this section, when the term whiteboard is used, it should be understood that it can be dry-erase or an electronic version.

Materials: Vocabulary list or questions, whiteboards, dry-erase markers and rags or erasers, or tablets/laptops

Application 1: For Vocabulary Practice

When students are first learning vocabulary you can say the word to them in the target language and have them illustrate it and write it down in the target language. Alternatively, you may wait until students have practiced the vocabulary and are more familiar and use this as a formative assessment. Ask students to hold up their board when they have finished their answers so you can check their work. By illustrating the word, students show you that they know what the word means. When having them write the word, you can help them sound it out and work with spelling patterns if necessary. Encourage them to have their vocabulary list out on their desk in case they can't remember the word at all or are confused by its spelling. Engage their thought processes more by asking them to think about what they remember of the word first before they just copy it from their vocabulary sheet.

Application 2: For Translation Practice

Whiteboards also work well for vocabulary and sentence translations. Give students a word or phrase in English and ask them to provide you with the same word or phrase in the target language.

Application 3: For Conjugation Practice

Students also enjoy using the whiteboards to practice conjugations. Give them a subject and a verb and ask them to give you the correct conjugation. Ask them to write out the whole conjugation chart for a verb in the mood and tense you are studying. Have students translate a verb phrase from English to the target language as well.

Application 4: For Question and Answer Practice

Have students practice question and answer formation using the whiteboards. Ask them to translate a question from English, answer one in the target language, or figure out the question from an answer you provide in the target language.

Application 5: For Cultural and Content Review

Use the whiteboards to review any cultural or content-based information. Determine topics you would like to review and give students questions to respond to, true or false statements, and fill-in-the-blank-type statements.

Butcher Paper

Butcher paper has many purposes. Butcher paper is a neutral colored paper that you can roll out into a large space on which students can draw or write. Allow students to work on the activity alone or in small groups. Once they have created their drawing and/or writing piece, ask them to give an oral presentation of their work to the class. Don't forget to take pictures of their work to save for subsequent years or to use in class for writing or oral discussion prompts.

Butcher Paper Sources

Butcher paper can be found through your school supplies catalogue and from other online sources. Butcher paper comes in brown and white. You can find other similar paper, usually a little more expensive and wider in width, by searching dual surface rolls, heavyweight craft paper roll, or banner paper. Different catalogues seem to use different names. The banner paper tends to be more expensive.

Ways to Use Butcher Paper

- Identify the important vocabulary from the unit, and draw and label it. Display the pictures on the walls of the classroom or in the hallway.

- Divide the paper into four sections, one for each season. Then illustrate and label weather and activities that fit the season in each quadrant.

- Trace another student's body and label the parts.

- Draw and label a house. Include common items found in each room. Then write sentences to identify what is in each room, or write a story about the house and the people who live in it.

- Draw a display window from a clothing store. Draw mannequins wearing a variety of different clothing and label the clothing with price tags. Write sentences about the cost and styles of the clothing or write about a shopping trip.

- Draw and label a neighborhood, town, or city. The students can draw their city or design an ideal one. Write about the area with sentences or a story.

- Draw and label a table set for a special dinner. Write about it.

- Draw and/or write out a story map, and then write a group story.

- Make a collage with pictures from magazines or from other sources. Write about the items included or the collage's significance.

- Draw a mural. Students vote on the best one(s) from the class, and it stays on the wall of the class or goes in the hallway for the month (or longer).

- Do a rendition of a Salvador Dalí painting or another artist's work.

- Design and create a game that can be played in a small group.

- Write a group story on the paper to display on your wall or in the hallway.

- Have students follow and complete a set of instructions for a task given in the target language. It could be a task like those previously described or something else. If you want to create a little competition, tell the class that the winner is the group that works most effectively together and produces the most accurate work the fastest. Provide a prize if you like.

Extension Activities With Butcher Paper

Extension 1: Have students present their work to the whole class. Adjust the length of the presentation based on skill levels and purpose. This works well if it was a group effort, as there will be fewer presentations. Alternatively, students can present their work to small groups and then get more practice by having to present it more than once.

Extension 2: Ask students to treat their work as a piece of artwork. Ask them to write a description for it to accompany the work and turn it in to put on the wall next to their work. Alternatively, ask students to take a digital picture of their work, which they can include with their written description. They can post the description and picture on a class blog, share on a class social media site like Edmodo, share it with you in Google Docs, or turn in a hard copy.

Extension 3: Building on Extension 2, students could also record a copy of their description with a free web-based service like www.vocaroo.com. Students could post their picture on the blog with or without the text and include the link to the audio. If students post the pictures on a wall, a QR code that students could scan using a QR code reader on their phone or tablet could be used to hear the audio.

Graphic Organizers

Graphic organizers are excellent tools that can facilitate various activities in any classroom.

Graphic Organizer Sources

If you are looking for graphic organizers, you may find it very helpful to talk to your colleagues in other content areas, especially language arts or social studies, depending on what your students are studying. Using common language and terminology across disciplines helps students make connections from one content area to another. Use as much of the same terminology as you can in the organizer or rubric.

It is also a wise idea to explore the wealth of great graphic organizers available online before creating your own and/or to get ideas on how to improve your own. Use your favorite search engine in your target language. If you use Google, type in Google Germany, for example. Click on the link and then put in the type of organizer you are looking for. Your results should come up in German. You can take a look at the results and also explore the Images section. Download and save resources you would like to use as they are or adapt for your class.

Ways to Use Graphic Organizers

- Tables for bingo boards

- Tables to collect information for pair activities and walk-around activities

- Tables to provide consistently sized boxes to make game cards for games like Memory and Go Fish cards, as well as vocabulary puzzle pieces

- Tables to organize subject pronouns, verb conjugations, reflexive pronouns, and other grammatical structures for note taking

- Tables and other graphic organizers to make important information stand out on the page and give the information a visual structure

- Graphic organizers to help when creating research guides; with a table you can use the first column to indicate the topic, the second for the information, and the third for making connections or determining the effect of the information.

- Venn diagrams to compare and contrast any information

- Tables to organize rubrics; www.rubistar.com is a place you may want to reference if you are creating rubrics.

- Graphic organizers to map story development when discussing literature

- Storyboards to help students visually and textually organize narrative writing that involves illustrations and movie scripts, as well as other relevant projects; allow students to search for their own or provide one.

Student Organizational Tools

Packets

One certainty of teaching is that students will be absent. Putting the list of key unit questions, vocabulary, grammar notes, and homework sheets all together in one packet for each unit can be a great time-saving measure and stress reducer. Using packets cuts down on time when students are looking for a homework sheet they missed from last week or when a parent calls and wants the homework because their child is or will be absent. Save time by having the students staple and three-hole-punch their own packets at the beginning of each unit. Make a few extra copies by asking a couple of students to go through the line twice to make extra packets for students who might lose one along the way, and store them in a student-accessible location. Help students stay organized by color-coding the sheets that go in the packet so they know what must be kept at the end of each unit. You may want to make the key questions sheet one color, vary the vocabulary sheets by unit, and make grammar notes sheets green (for grammar) and homework sheets white. At the end of each unit it is helpful to let students know that they must keep all their colored sheets; they may choose to recycle the white homework sheets or keep them to review. Any other important reference handouts are also printed on color so students know to keep them.

If your school uses Google Apps for Education, you can share resources with students electronically using Google Drive or Google Classroom. Classroom allows you to post and collect assignments, as well as post announcements and other resources. If you do this, you will want to consider ahead of time which materials you may want to provide a printed copy of—for example, vocabulary sheets, key reference materials like standard rubrics, study suggestions, listening activities, etc. You will want to make your decisions based upon the access your students have to technology both at school and at home. Also, you will want to consider how your students best learn and provide a mix of technology and paper-based resources to allow flexibility and provide varied modes of practice. Also, consider replacing some worksheets with interactive online practice, using sites like www.quizlet.com, www.quia.com (flashcards and games), www.conjuguemos.com (conjugation and vocabulary practice), www.textivate.com (varied games and comprehension questions), and www.eclipsecrossword.com (crossword puzzle creator). Many of the sites have free or some free and some paid resources.

Binders

Having students use binders for class is useful in the world language classroom. Binders can be divided for different topics and are helpful for storing reference materials in an orderly fashion. They are particularly helpful if you have a lot of class handouts.

The Daily Classroom Binder

Use the Daily Classroom Binder to keep a record of notes, classroom activities, homework assignments, and upcoming test announcements from each class. Ask a reliable student to fill in the information on the record sheets you keep in the binder every day. Let students know that when they have been absent, the binder is the first place they should go to find out what they missed. This saves both you and the students time at the beginning of the class period.

Online Calendars and Blogs

You may want to consider using an online calendar to share information with students and parents. If you are using Google Apps, you may want to use its calendar. You may also have a school website that has a similar feature. You can embed a Google calendar in your class website that will update as you update the homework, tests, holidays, or other events you may want to share with students and parents. Blogs are also a nice resource to provide parents and students who may be absent with a synopsis of the week's events. Depending upon the purpose of the blog, you may have a student recap the week and be the guest blogger, or you can provide a quick update and any information on important upcoming events. Some blogs or websites with blog features you may want to consider are: www.weebly.com, www.edublogs.com, and www.wordpress.com. Your school website may also already have this feature available.

The Student Station

Create a table or area in the class where student supplies, such as scissors, crayons and markers, extra pencils, tape, a stapler, a hole punch, and so forth, are kept. This way students know that they can just go there, use the item, and return it. Having such a location allows students easier access to materials and reduces the number of questions you answer about supplies.

Learning About Your Students

Determining Your Students' Learning Styles

First and foremost, write lesson plans—including activities—that take into consideration the diverse learning styles of your students. During the course of a week's lessons, do your best to engage all student learning styles. Use songs, drawings, and vocabulary picture and word flashcards; get kids out of their desks and moving around; use gestures and actions for teaching vocabulary whenever possible; and provide many opportunities for pair and group oral language practice, as well as quiet activities that allow students to read and write in the target language. Encourage students to listen to music and watch television and movies in the target language during their free time.

Strategies to Help Determine Your Students' Learning Styles

Strategy 1: Observe Your Students' Reactions

Observe your students' reactions to your instructional style and activities. Certain classes may prefer general instructional strategies over others. Be flexible and adjust accordingly. If one class enjoys acting out vocabulary and another doesn't, be prepared to substitute activities. It may seem like a lot of extra planning, but it can be as simple as allowing one class to act out a mini-story that you ad-lib, whereas another class quizzes vocabulary one-on-one in pairs or maybe plays a short game of Pictionary. Get in the habit of writing lesson plans with a couple of alternative activities at the bottom that accomplish the same goal in a different way. Students appreciate it, and you will, too, because you can keep the group more engaged and as a result may have fewer class disruptions.

Strategy 2: Survey Your Students

Another way to determine learning styles is to have students fill out a survey on which you list particular activities you use in class. Ask your students to rank the activities from one to five, with five being representative of the activities that are most useful in helping students remember the material. Collect the data and pick out trends in the class to help you adjust instruction. Try using a survey like this at the very beginning of the year when you first meet new students and again at various points during the year, once students become more familiar with your activities.

Strategy 3: Give Your Students a Multiple Intelligences Questionnaire

Give students one of the many learning styles questionnaires that are online or in other resource books. The surveys find overall trends and give you a sense of the students' strengths. Paying attention to learning styles and varying your instruction to include activities that appeal to a variety of your students throughout your class period or throughout the week improve the level of engagement in and retention of the material your students are learning.

Collecting Student Feedback About Class

Having open communication lines with students about how your teaching and instructional activities are working for them is essential. There are various ways to go about collecting feedback—for example, informal individual or group conversations in which you just ask students how something worked for them, anonymous (or not) surveys on paper, and online surveys. One online survey that works nicely for anonymous, well-organized feedback is www.zoomerang.com. It has both free and paid options. Google Forms also work nicely for collecting student feedback. Opening up the dialogue about learning and asking students for constructive feedback help create a culture of collaboration and give you a much better sense of how things are working for your students.

Promoting and Monitoring Class Participation

Question Randomizer Tools

There are many tools to help you engage a variety of students in class participation to avoid calling on the same students all of the time. One that serves more than one purpose is an index card. At the beginning of the year, have students fill out an index card with some personal information, including first and last name; if they have siblings and pets; their favorite food, color, animal, vacation, and so forth; and one thing they want to learn in class this year. Use the information to get to know the students a little better. Once you have this information, you can also use it to ask the class questions to see how well they know one another. (Who has a dog named Skippy? Who has been to Puerto Rico?)

On the reverse side of the same index card, have the students write their name in the target language, if you allow them to choose names. Use the cards to call on students randomly during homework review or other group questioning activities. Make sure to shuffle used cards back into the middle of the deck somewhere, not the end; otherwise students stop paying attention after they have been called on once. Using the cards keeps kids more focused because they never know when they might get called on to answer. It also speeds up the process of checking homework because you don't need to decide whom to call on next. Occasionally, ask for students to volunteer to answer questions.

Other tools for calling on students include low- to high-tech options. Popsicle sticks with student names in a can or bag organized by class are a simple but handy option. Interactive whiteboard software SMART Notebook has a tool to randomly select students, as well as group them; https://www.superteachertools.net/ has one, as well as other helpful tools. Apps are also available by searching random name selector or generator.

Student Participation Self-Assessment Rubric

Involve students in assessing their own behavior and participation to help them become more aware of how their choices affect their use of class time. Figure 1.1 is a self-assessment rubric that students fill out about themselves on a weekly or biweekly basis. It is set up using an E for excellent, S for satisfactory, and U for unsatisfactory. As you read the students' self-assessments, determine if you agree with them. If you do not, circle the area in which you believe they are performing. You can use the rubric as a tool to discuss behavioral problems with the students who are showing a pattern of them and reinforce the positive effort of other students. You could hold on to the self-assessments for all students for conferences or limit what you keep to students who have developed a

Directions: After reading the category descriptions, circle the box that best represents your level of participation in each of the categories.

	Effort	Use of Spanish	Behavior
	I participated in class this week by . . .	In class I . . .	During class I . . .
E	putting forth good effort when doing actions, drawings, writing, and when singing. I did all pair and group activities well. I frequently raised my hand to contribute to class.	used the Spanish words I have learned, rather than the English ones. I accomplished this by using classroom expressions, greeting the teacher and others in Spanish, using only the Spanish questions and expressions during pair and group activities, and using Spanish vocabulary I have learned whenever possible.	do not disrupt class and always raise my hand when I have questions that are relevant to class. I do not talk when the teacher is instructing class or while other students are speaking during instructional activities.
S	putting forth an average effort when doing individual, pair, and group activities. I sometimes raised my hand to contribute to class.	used the Spanish words I have learned most of the time.	do not disrupt class more than once a week.
U	putting forth a minimal effort when doing individual, pair, and group activities. I didn't raise my hand much to contribute to class.	do not use the Spanish classroom expressions or other vocabulary learned in class to improve my ability to speak in Spanish.	disrupt class by blurting out instead of raising my hand and/or talking while the teacher is instructing class. I may make comments that have nothing to do with the topic of the day that disrupt the teacher and the rest of the class.

Figure 1.1 Student Participation Self-Assessment Rubric

© *Activities, Games, and Assessment Strategies for the World Language Classroom*, Amy Buttner Zimmer, Taylor & Francis

pattern of behavioral issues. This could provide you with concrete information to discuss with the student and their parent(s) for problem-solving purposes.

Rubric for Target Language Activities

Use the rubric in Figure 1.2 to monitor student participation in target language activities. Although the simplest way to monitor students is informally by circulating around the room and listening to or visually checking any written work, some students need a formal system to keep them on track. However, you can also use it as a way to collect more concrete data on formative student progress. Some students need to know that their work is being assessed or they will not demonstrate their best effort. Use this rubric to assess the students' participation based on their completion of the activity, use of the target language, comprehension of the activity, and communication during the activity. You can also just assess a couple categories each time during an activity.

Also following the rubric is a class participation assessment record sheet (Figure 1.3) on which you can record student participation data. This rubric is flexible and can be used to monitor oral and written activities. You can use it to provide a concrete basis for a participation grade. In most circumstances you should not expect to evaluate all students during one activity. The assessment is most effective when students are given a copy of the rubric as well as an explanation of your expectations. Make your evaluations random so students do not know when they are being evaluated. You can use the rubric and record sheet to track a student's effort and participation for formative purposes to provide you with more information about the student's progress and effort to share with students and parents. You could, however, also use the rubric for a summative assessment, focusing in on the use of the target language, comprehension, and communication.

Charting Negative Behaviors to Decrease Disruptions

The best way to get student cooperation and participation in class is to build a good relationship with them by showing genuine interest in them and being empathetic. Some unnecessary conflicts arise between students and teachers because a teacher misinterprets a situation and reacts, making the student defensive. Try to first ask the student what is going on before making an assumption and rushing to judgment. That being said, it is still important to have a clear set of expectations and a way to monitor and record student participation and progress in class activities. Have a predetermined system of expectations, as well as consequences for interruptions or failure to complete activities. A short, simple list of behavior expectations is easier for students to remember and for you to enforce. Although there are many different systems that teachers use to monitor student progress and behavior, the key factor is your willingness to consistently and fairly use the system. You may want to involve the students in discussing what they want their class to look like and have them help create the expectations and consequences. Doing this usually results in the same expectations you would have identified, but provides students with an opportunity to have a voice in the conversation and be more invested in the expectations.

There are many ways to monitor student behavior, and the system needs to take into account your particular group of students and your teaching style. One system for charting behavior I have used (Figure 1.4) is to write down the name of the student having the behavior problem and put hash marks behind their name for repeated occurrences on your own paper. The act of writing down their name can be a deterrent to most behaviors, as long as they know there is a consequence. It also is less disruptive than having to verbally address the student. Charting the behaviors also provides a very valuable log of information about them if you need to discuss a behavioral issue that has become a pattern with the student, a parent, or an administrator. When you feel like a pattern

Rubric for Target Language Activities	E	S	U	Rating
Task Completion	• Has listened to directions and knows how to complete the task. • Begins the activity right away and easily finishes in the allotted time.	• Needs a reminder to begin the activity. • Barely finishes the activity in the allotted time.	• Is not prepared to begin the activity on time because he/she did not pay attention. • Does not finish the activity during the allotted time because of a lack of focus.	
Use of Target Language	• Uses only the target language for all pair communication during the activity. • Uses expressions like: *Please repeat, I don't understand, What?* if he/she needs to hear the question again.	• Uses the required amount of the target language to complete the activity. • Uses the expressions: *Please repeat, I don't understand*, etc., to ask for help.	• Talks to friends instead of working. • Asks and answers the questions in English.	
Comprehension	• Student comprehends the questions and answers given by the other students.	• Student does not always comprehend the questions and answers from other students, but asks them clarification questions to find out.	• Student does not comprehend the question and/or answer and makes no attempt to find it out.	
Communication	• Student communication goes beyond the scope of the activity.	• Student successfully communicates with his/her partner.	• Student makes no effort to communicate with his/her partner.	

Figure 1.2 Rubric for Target Language Activities

Assessment Record for Target Language Activities	Evaluation Period 1				Evaluation Period 2				Evaluation Period 3			
	Task Completion	Use of Target Language	Comprehension	Communication	Task Completion	Use of Target Language	Comprehension	Communication	Task Completion	Use of Target Language	Comprehension	Communication
Berner, Katie	S	S	S	S	S	S	S	S	S	S	S	S
Cristoff, Emily	E	E	E	E	E	E	E	E	E	E	E	E
Krueger, Casey	U	U	U	U	S	S	S	S	S	S	S	S
Matthews, Morgan	S	S	S	S	E	E	E	S	S	S	S	S
Sorens, Will	S	S	S	S	S	S	S	S	S	S	S	S
Williams, John	U	U	U	U	U	U	U	U	S	S	S	S

Figure 1.3 Assessment Record for Target Language Activities
(Note: The downloadable version is blank so you can add your own students' names.)

of negative behavior is developing, repeated times on the chart in one day, or over a couple days, would be the time to address the issue. A good starting point is to simply talk to the student and try to resolve the problem without detentions or getting a parent involved. Discussing the issue and having the student propose a realistic solution to the problem whenever possible are ideal. Keeping the focus on building the relationship with the student and finding the cause of the behavior, rather than just addressing the behavior with a quick solution, are a good starting point. If the problem persists, another conversation with the student is warranted and, depending upon how you feel about the conversation, a detention, reflection, or parent phone call may be warranted. If a phone call home is necessary, consider asking the student to take ownership of the problem by calling his or her parents and explaining what he or she did. Make sure to talk with the parent immediately after the student finishes the conversation so you can also explain any missing information or answer questions. If the problem persists, a sit-down meeting with you, the student, and your building administrator, if possible, may be a next step. Another option is always informing the principal of the situation via email and asking that he or she speak with the student. These would be for situations that are more disruptive or disrespectful, rather than dangerous. For those, follow your building protocol. Having a student step out of class is also an alternative if you are too upset with the student to interact with or speak to him or her about the situation.

For instances in which more than a few students are taking too much time to settle down or not responding to instructions, the "time after the bell" column of the chart can be used. When you greet students or redirect them to a new activity you can wait about 5 seconds and then expect that their conversations have ended. If they are still talking, you can use the strategy of simply starting to stare at the clock and counting the time that goes by until someone notices. However long it takes them to stop is how long you keep them after the bell. Generally, it does not take very long for a student to notice that you are watching the clock. Students tend to settle each other down because they do not want to stay after the bell. As educators we teach in a wide array of instructional settings, and there is no one simple plan for classroom management that will work for everyone. Ultimately the best behavioral plan is based on mutual respect and relationship building and includes the steps and consequences that work best for you and for your students.

Day:			Date:		
	Time After Bell	**Behavioral Issues**			
		Blurts Out/ Disrupts Instruction	**Talking to Others During Instructional Time**	**Disrespect Toward Others**	**Other**
Hour 1					
Hour 2					
Hour 3					
Hour 4					
Hour 5					
Hour 6					
Hour 7					
Hour 8					

Figure 1.4 Daily Classroom Behavior Chart

2

Strategies to Promote and Assess Oral Proficiency

Classroom Survival Language

Classroom Survival Expressions

Take the time to collect or create a list of classroom survival expressions or *Phrases of the Day.* Although you may write one on the board each day for students to copy down into a notebook, students appreciate having a premade list of them. This way, students don't have to wait until November to learn a particular expression they might like to have now. It also facilitates review of past expressions, because you can ask students to take out the expression-of-the-day packet for a quick review. Flashcards of the expressions are helpful, too. Make a list for each level so students continue to learn new expressions. These lists may also come in handy for students when they write dialogues.

Classroom Survival Posters

From your survival expressions list, choose the most important of the expressions and involve interested students in designing and illustrating the expressions on a poster. Invite them to use online tools or their own artistic abilities to create them. Two online tools to try out are http://phrase.it/ and http://www.superlame.com/. Search for others by looking for an online speech bubble editor. Students will enjoy seeing their work on the wall, and their involvement in creating them will help them remember the expressions.

Key Unit Questions

Writing the Questions

At the beginning of each unit, brainstorm a list of key unit questions you feel are essential for students to be able to ask and answer. Depending upon your teaching style, either determine your list of them and type them up to give to your students or have your students generate a collective list they would want to be able to use. You can type the list right into a Google Doc that you can then share with your students or use a different word processing program and print a list. Make sure students understand upfront how they will be assessed and that the purpose for needing to know the questions is identified. The following activities help students practice the questions for your assessment. Some of the activities can also double as the assessment at the end of the unit.

Sample Questions for a Unit on Shopping for Clothing

- What do you need to buy?
- Do you want to go shopping with me on Saturday?
- Do you prefer the red or blue shirt?
- Do you like my new coat?
- Where did you buy it?

- How does it fit me?
- What do you think of these pants?
- Should I buy them?
- How much is it?

Practicing the Questions

Class Challenge

Materials: Key unit questions written on index cards

Write the key questions on 3 × 5 cards. Write one question per card. At various points during the week, have a volunteer student come up to the front of the class and conduct a Class Challenge. The student questioner can pick anyone in the class to answer the question on the card. If the student answers the question correctly, the class gets a point. If not, the questioner gets the point. Determine ahead of time how many points you will play. Initially, the questioner generally tends to win, but as the unit progresses, the class usually does. An alternative if you have the questions typed up in www.quizlet.com is to print out the cards from one of their various options in the Print menu.

Pair and Group Activities

Materials: Varied pair activities

Make sure that the key questions are also included in pair and group practice activities. Information Gap activities lend themselves well to practicing these oral questions. Walk-around activities are also good because you can set up the activity so students can ask the same question multiple times of various students. You can also provide students with a scenario on paper or projected on the board as part of your warm-up. Scaffold the practice by initially providing the questions in the target language and the start of an answer if needed, or have them refer to their key question resource list. As students become more comfortable, remove the answers, then provide an answer so that they need to determine the question. By the end, provide a bullet point list of the questions in English or the topics to be discussed.

Ladders

Materials: Ladder sheet

At the beginning of each week, pass out a blank *ladder* to students (see Figure 2.1). Put the ladder in a table and put as many *rungs* on it as you want. For each rung, the students must ask each other a question in the target language. Once they ask the question, they can shade in the space between the rungs on the ladder. This activity works well at the beginning of the hour for students to practice their key questions or engage in other conversation. Encourage students to do more than one ladder a week if they are able to do so. It is a simple way to get students to practice current and previous essential questions on a regular basis. See the ladder on page 20 for an example.

Assessing the Questions

The following options offer some general varied suggestions for formative or summative oral assessment for students of different proficiency levels.

Option 1: Basic Oral Questioning

Before the assessment, prepare by writing all of your key questions on index cards, one question per card (or by printing them from Quizlet). Also, plan your lesson so students are able to work on independent, pair, or small group work that does not require your assistance. Consider designating a student as the go-to person for questions. You will be having students come to you individually for their assessment. Also, make sure your students have seen the rubric and have had a chance to work with it in a formative assessment experience before the summative. You can use the rubric in Figure 2.2 or a similar one to assess students' answers

When a student comes to be assessed, ask him or her to pick two or three cards from the cards that you have lying face down. Students prefer the opportunity to choose their cards even when they don't know exactly what questions they will get. Ask the student to pass the cards to you face down so he or she can't peek at the questions. Ask the student the questions and record the scores. A spreadsheet is useful for recording scores from each category and for calculating subtotals and final scores. Use the scores from the individual categories to provide feedback to your students about their strengths and areas for improvement. See Figure 2.3 for an example spreadsheet.

Option 2: Conversational Oral Test

Sit down with 2–3 students and create more of a conversation atmosphere for your questions. Create a rotation where each student is the first to answer 2–3 questions during the course of the conversation. Once the student answers the "new" question, the other students in the group also provide their answer to the question. Once each student has a chance to answer the first question, then the second student in the rotation answers the next question, but is first in doing so. The rotation continues like this until the questions have been answered. You can adjust your questioning based on the needs of the students, offering either/or answers or some options if they struggle, while leaving questions more open-ended for students who can handle them. You will want to have a laptop or tablet where students are not able to see what you are marking down as you evaluate. This can be a very enjoyable way of oral testing because it feels more conversation-like.

Option 3: Dialogue

Create a situation that requires students to create a dialogue that integrates the key questions from your unit. Traditionally, dialogues are performed for the whole class. This has the potential of being very repetitive (unless that is your purpose). An alternative is to have activities students can be engaged in doing independently or in small groups while you have students perform their dialogues for you without the class audience. This can be beneficial for students who get anxious in front of small groups or are early language learners, or if you want to be able to give students immediate, timely feedback. This option is nice because it makes the feedback more personal, saves you time in writing all of the feedback, and allows students to easily ask any questions. Students can, of course, record dialogues, which can be nice for a project. When students have to converse with you or a partner in person, though, it allows you to get a better sense of what they can perform live. See the "Assessing the Quick Chats" section of this chapter for ideas on how to help scaffold students to help them have extended dialogues.

Option 4: Impromptu Situations

Provide students with a situation the day of the assessment that requires that they integrate the key questions and vocabulary from the unit. You may or may not give them a few minutes to think about what they might want to say. This will have them thinking more on their feet, as they would have to do in a real situation, as we never quite know

Finish		Finish		Finish		Finish	
	38		38		38		38
	37		37		37		37
	36		36		36		36
	35		35		35		35
	34		34		34		34
	33		33		33		33
	32		32		32		32
	31		31		31		31
	30		30		30		30
	29		29		29		29
	28		28		28		28
	27		27		27		27
	26		26		26		26
	25		25		25		25
	24		24		24		24
	23		23		23		23
	22		22		22		22
	21		21		21		21
	20		20		20		20
	19		19		19		19
	18		18		18		18
	17		17		17		17
	16		16		16		16
	15		15		15		15
	14		14		14		14
	13		13		13		13
	12		12		12		12
	11		11		11		11
	10		10		10		10
	9		9		9		9
	8		8		8		8
	7		7		7		7
	6		6		6		6
	5		5		5		5
	4		4		4		4
	3		3		3		3
	2		2		2		2
	1		1		1		1

Figure 2.1 Ladder Sheet

Oral Questioning Rubric	2	1	0
Comprehensibility/ Content	• The student provides a comprehensible, complete response that indicates understanding of the question(s). • The student may make an attempt to give a more elaborate response.	• The student provides a basic but comprehensible response. • The response may be a correct answer, but it is incomplete. • The teacher may have to repeat or rephrase the question(s) once.	• The student does not understand the question and cannot answer it even after the teacher has slowly repeated it twice.
Fluency	• The student gives a fluid response.	• The student pauses or hesitates, but the listener still comprehends.	• The student speaks haltingly with excessively long pauses that detract from the listener's ability to comprehend.
Accuracy	• There are minimal to no grammatical errors. • The student will self-correct any conjugation errors. • The student uses the correct words to express what he/she is saying.	• There are some grammatical errors, but the student is still comprehensible. • The student uses the correct verb for the meaning he/she wants to convey, but the grammatical use is incorrect. • The student may use a vocabulary word incorrectly, but the intended meaning is still understood from the context.	• Grammatical errors are so frequent that the student is no longer comprehensible. • The student cannot figure out what verb should be used to answer. • The student uses several words incorrectly.
Pronunciation	• The student correctly pronounces all or almost all of the words in the response.	• The student pronounces most of the words in the answer correctly.	• The student mispronounces all or almost all of the words in the response.

Figure 2.2 Key Oral Questioning Rubric

how a conversation will go ahead of time in most cases. See more about how to build students up to working with impromptu situations through the use of role-plays later in the chapter.

Data-Tracking Tools

A spreadsheet is an excellent tool for tracking data about student performance. Although most teachers now have electronic grade books to collect data and tabulate grades, spreadsheets can provide a format to gather more specific data. Track data on individual students for each category of a rubric for written and oral work samples. The individual categories of assessment on the spreadsheet help identify areas of improvement for specific individuals and help you give them more precise feedback. Over time this tracking method shows trends and may also help you identify areas for instructional improvement if many students have low scores in a particular area.

Speaking Prompts

Writing the Quick Chat Prompts

Make quick chat prompt cards so students can practice the questions they ask one another on a regular basis. Try to focus your quick chat prompts on language students frequently use with one another, their friends, and their families. Students will be much more apt to use the target language when they can use it to talk about things that are important to them and that they commonly discuss on a daily basis. See the following questions for some ideas.

1. What are you going to do tonight?
2. Are you going anywhere this weekend?
3. Do you have plans on Saturday? Would you like to do something with me?
4. Do you want to go to a movie with me on Sunday afternoon?
5. What did you do over the weekend?
6. Did you do anything fun last night?
7. Where did you go on Friday night? What did you do?

Figure 2.4 illustrates one way to format the Quick Chat Prompt card.

Source: Adapted from *Developing Speaking and Writing Tasks,* Minnesota Language Proficiency Assessments, p. 17, www.carla.umn.edu/assessment/MLPA/pdfs/miniguide.pdf.

Assessing the Quick Chats

Pass the cards out to your paired students on Monday with the question in the target language. Take some time to model responses or ensure students have previously worked with this material and are comfortable with options for responses. Explain that they need to take turns asking their partner the question on the card. Each partner should be able to ask and answer the question in the target language. One student begins by asking his or her

	Question 1					Question 2					Question 3					
	Comprehensibility	Fluency	Accuracy	Pronunciation	Subtotal 1	Comprehensibility	Fluency	Accuracy	Pronunciation	Subtotal 2	Comprehensibility	Fluency	Accuracy	Pronunciation	Subtotal 3	Total / 24
Sara Bender	2	2	1	2	7	2	2	2	2	8	2	2	1	2	7	22
Mark Carmichael	1	2	1	2	6	2	2	1	2	7	2	1	1	1	5	18
John Dolan	2	2	2	2	8	2	2	2	2	8	2	2	2	2	8	24
Peter O'Leary	1	1	2	2	6	2	1	2	2	7	1	2	1	2	6	19
Pedro Velasquez	2	2	2	2	8	2	2	2	2	8	2	2	2	2	8	24
Total Possible	**2**	**2**	**2**	**2**	**8**	**2**	**2**	**2**	**2**	**8**	**2**	**2**	**2**	**2**	**8**	**24**

Oral Questioning Assessment: Food   **Date:** 5/31/07

Figure 2.3 Oral Questioning Data-Tracking Sheet

Prompt: Ask your partner what he/she wants to do tonight.

Name of partner answering:_____

Name of evaluator:_____

Score	My partner
5	o Said at least 5 sentences about the topic, using a variety of details. o Sounded fluid in his or her response with few hesitations.
4	o Said 3 or 4 sentences about the topic with some details.
3	o Sounded mostly fluid in his or her response with some hesitations.
2	o Said 1 or 2 sentences about the topic with little to no details.
1	o Had a lot of hesitations that were distracting in his or her response.
/5	Total

Figure 2.4 Quick Chat Prompt Card

partner the question. The partner should be able to respond with five statements in response to the question. Give your students a little time at the beginning of the hour each day to practice, and remind students to use the question with their partner and classmates as the week progresses. Listen to the student conversations to get formative assessment data on students' oral responses.

Plan to listen to a portion of your class each week while the rest of the class works on an in-class activity. If you are concerned about not hearing each student talk about each question, loop similar questions back in to be practiced in subsequent weeks. Although the students are only evaluating each other based on the number of sentences they hear and how fluid the response sounds, the teacher evaluation can include additional areas of assessment. Determine if you want to assess the students for progress or assign a grade. You may use the ESU scale if you would like to give feedback on progress and not record a grade. If you are not going to record a grade for the students, still consider recording the ESU so you can track their progress. See the rubric and data-tracking sheet for the Quick Chat Prompts that follow for further explanation (Figures 2.5, 2.6, and 2.7).

Writing and Assessing Role-Plays

Provide students with situation cards like the following ones that describe a role to play (Figure 2.8). Use the cards to give students oral and written language practice. Ask the students to use the outline on the card as a framework from which they create a dialogue. Students can do the dialogue as informal pair practice or for a performance for you and/or the class. Adapt how you use the situation cards, depending on student ability level and the amount of practice they have already had with the material. Remind students to make use of their key unit questions as well as other relevant lessons on vocabulary. See the sample rubric for assessing dialogues (Figure 2.9).

A general speaking rubric that you may find to be valuable is from Scott Benedict of www.teachforjune.com (Figure 2.10).

Strategies to Encourage the Use of the Target Language

General Thoughts

First and foremost, make sure that you are consistently using the target language if you would like your students to speak it. Begin the process of asking the students to use the target language slowly over a period of time so they are not overwhelmed. Once you have taught the survival expressions, ask the students to always use those with you and others. As students learn new vocabulary in the target language, ask that they use those words instead of the English equivalent. If students use English for words you know they have learned in Spanish, politely tell them you don't understand and ask for the word, phrase, or question in the target language. When doing pair and group activities with questions, explain that the students are expected to speak only in the target language for the time it takes to do the activity and that they are evaluated on their use of it.

It is also useful to have a system in place to reinforce the use of the target language. Any of the following systems tend to work better if there are points attached to them for a student speaking grade. As you decide which system to use, the most important factor is whether you feel comfortable with it and can consistently apply it. Monitor how your students are responding to the systems. Sometimes a combination of a couple methods or switching from one system to another at the beginning of a new grading period may be helpful.

	Proficient 6.0 5.5	Basic 5.0	Minimal 4.5 4.0	Score /24
Content/ Comprehensibility	• The student provides a comprehensible, detailed response that demonstrates understanding of the question. • The response is five or more sentences long.	• The student provides a basic, but comprehensible, response that demonstrates understanding of the question. • The response answers the question, but not as completely or with as much detail as a proficient student. • The student may not be able to provide the full five sentences required of the more complete response.	• The student provides a response, but it lacks completeness and details. • The response is three or fewer sentences long.	/6
Accuracy	• There are minimal or no grammatical errors. • The student may self-correct his or her errors.	• Grammatical errors are more noticeable, but the student is still comprehensible. • Some errors in verb conjugations, noun-adjective agreement, etc. typical of his or her developmental level are present.	• The student does not consistently conjugate verbs correctly. Noun-adjective agreement and other grammatical errors are also problematic. • The grammatical errors are beginning to distract the listener from the meaning of the communication.	/6
Fluency	• The student gives a fluid response. Any pauses in speech do not detract from the response. • Sentences are more complex, not short and choppy.	• Some sentences may be fluid, but others may have more distracting pauses and hesitations. • Some of the sentences may begin to sound short and choppy.	• The student speaks haltingly with excessively long pauses that detract from the listener's ability to follow what the student is trying to communicate. • The sentences are mostly short and choppy.	/6
Pronunciation	• The student has highly accurate pronunciation.	• The student correctly pronounces most of the words in the answer.	• The student mispronounces many of the words in the answer.	/6

Figure 2.5 Quick Chat Rubric

Quick Chats Record Sheet	Date: October 7th					Date: October 14th					Date: October 21st				
	Content	Accuracy	Fluency	Pronunciation	TOTAL	Content	Accuracy	Fluency	Pronunciation	TOTAL	Content	Accuracy	Fluency	Pronunciation	TOTAL
Sara Bender	6	5.5	6	5.5	23						6	6	6	6	24
Mark Carmichael	4.5	5	4.5	4.5	18.5						5	5	5	5	20
Nicole Hoffman						6	6	6	6	24					
Peter O'Leary						4	4	4.5	5	17.5					
Angela Sutton	5.5	6	5	4.5	21						5.5	5.5	5	5	21
Pedro Velasquez						6	5	5.5	5.5	22					
Total	6	6	6	6	24	6	6	6	6	24	6	6	6	6	24

Figure 2.6 Quick Prompts Data-Tracking Sheet

Quick Chat Prompts Record Sheet	Date: October 7th				Date: October 14th				Date: October 21st			
	Content	Accuracy	Fluency	Pronunciation	Content	Accuracy	Fluency	Pronunciation	Content	Accuracy	Fluency	Pronunciation
Sara Bender	P	P	P	P								
Mark Carmichael	M	B	M	M					B	B	B	B
Nicole Hoffman												
John Dolan					P	P	P	P				
Peter O'Leary					M	M	M	B				
Angela Sutton	P	P	B	M					P	P	B	B
Pedro Velasquez					P	B	P	P				

Figure 2.7 Quick Chats Record Sheet: Proficiency Scoring

A

Making and answering a phone call

You want to make plans with your friend. Call him/her at home to make plans.

♦ Greet your friend's sibling who answers the phone.

♦ Ask if your friend Carlos is home.

♦ Ask when he will return.

♦ Ask if you can leave a message.

♦ Leave a message asking him to call you when he gets back.

♦ Thank Carlos's sibling and say good-bye.

B

Making and answering a phone call

Your brother's friend calls to make some plans with your brother, but he is not home.

♦ Answer the phone when it rings.

♦ Tell the caller that your brother is not home.

♦ Tell his friend that you do not know when he will be back.

♦ Answer, "Yes, of course."

♦ Respond by saying good-bye.

Figure 2.8 Role-Play Cards

Dialogue and Role-Play Rubric	10.0 9.5	9.0 8.5	8.0 7.5	7.0 6.5	Total 60	Comments
Vocabulary/ Task completion	• All elements of the presentation are included. • Dialogue includes creative vocabulary that enhances it.	• All elements of the presentation are included. • Dialogue includes the required vocabulary and it is used correctly.	• Dialogue is only partially on topic and too brief. • Dialogue is missing some important vocabulary and/or it is used incorrectly.	• Students did not complete the task as assigned. • English is used. • Inappropriate or inadequate use of vocabulary.	10	
Comprehensibility	• Easy to understand. • No confusion of vocabulary words. • Listener does not need make any attempts to interpret what the speaker is saying because of lack of clarity. • Students respond appropriately to one another's questions.	• Dialogue is comprehensible. • The listener infrequently has to interpret what the speakers are saying because of lack of clarity. • Students respond appropriately to one another's questions; however, there may be some delay in response.	• Dialogue is choppy with parts that seem disconnected and are difficult to follow. • Some instances of students not being able to correctly respond to their partner's questions.	• Questions and responses barely comprehensible as evidenced by: • Confusion of vocabulary words. • Listener struggling to comprehend speakers. • Inability of students to respond to one another's questions.	10	
Fluency	• Dialogue is comfortably memorized so that there are few to no hesitations that break the flow of the dialogue. • Uses more complex sentences of varied lengths. • Sentences are not choppy.	• Hesitations break the flow of the dialogue at times, but do not interfere with comprehension. • Most sentences are complete, but they are not as varied.	• There are various hesitations that distract from the dialogue. • Some sentences are complete, whereas others are short and incomplete.	• Choppy because of frequent pauses in speech and/or incomplete thoughts. • Most sentences are fragmented and disconnected.	10	
Accuracy	• Few to no grammatical errors in communication. • Correct grammar aids in listener's comprehension of the dialogue.	• May make various grammatical errors, but they do not impede communication.	• Grammatical errors begin to impede listener's ability to understand the dialogue.	• High frequency of grammatical errors distract from listener's comprehension of dialogue.	10	
Pronunciation	• Pronunciation is clear. Few to no errors.	• Some errors, but still understandable.	• Errors begin to strongly hinder listener's ability to understand dialogue.	• High frequency of poorly pronounced words.	10	
Performance	• Creative touches add to the realism of the dialogue. • Lively presentation with appropriate changes in voice inflection. • Speaker is easy to hear.	• Some enthusiasm. • Generally appropriate changes in voice inflection applied to dialogue. • Speaker is easy to hear.	• Little enthusiasm. • Some changes in voice inflection used, but they may be inaccurate. • Speaker is not as easy to hear.	• No enthusiasm at all. • Presentation is done in monotone. • Speaker may be quite difficult to hear.	10	

Figure 2.9 Dialogue and Role-Play Rubric

© *Activities, Games, and Assessment Strategies for the World Language Classroom*, Amy Buttner Zimmer, Taylor & Francis

SPEAKING RUBRIC

An F grade will be earned if speaking fails to address task or is insufficient to make proper evaluation.	A	✓	**STUDENT CONSISTENTLY SPEAKS ABOVE INSTRUCTION LEVEL.** ☐ **SPEAKING** expands upon task with much detail, flows naturally using appropriate transitions, and with little hesitation; sentences are longer including uses of and/or/but and may include uses of because/since/therefore; ideas are fully developed and well organized; appropriate use of dialogue may be evident. ☐ **VOCABULARY** use exhibits an extensive range of both current and previous vocabulary with minimal errors. ☐ **STRUCTURES** are at upper tier of instruction; errors are minimal; pronunciation is accurate; consistent use of both basic-beginner and intermediate-beginner structures; emerging use of advanced-beginner structures (object pronouns, adjective agreement, ser/estar, preterite/imperfect, stem-changers, and irregular past/future forms).
	B	Meets Target	**STUDENT CONSISTENTLY SPEAKS AT INSTRUCTION LEVEL.** ☐ **SPEAKING** develops task fully with some detail and flows naturally; some hesitation is evident, but does not interfere with understanding; sentences are longer and may include uses of and/or/but; ideas are organized and developed. ☐ **VOCABULARY** use is adequate and appropriate to task with few errors and exhibits much use of current vocabulary; some previous vocabulary may be evident. ☐ **STRUCTURES** are appropriate to instruction; errors do not hinder overall comprehension; pronunciation errors are minimal; consistent use of basic-beginner structures; emergent use of intermediate-beginner structures (present/past/future, adjective position, irregular present forms, want to go/can write/has to study, reflexive verbs, gustar & similar verbs, and verbs after prepositions).
	C	Approaches Target	**STUDENT SOMETIMES SPEAKS AT INSTRUCTION LEVEL.** ☐ **SPEAKING** addresses task completely but is simple, lacking details; sentences may be choppy, but are organized and complete and may be merely a list of descriptions or actions. ☐ **VOCABULARY** use is limited and may be incorrect, but some current vocabulary is evident. ☐ **STRUCTURES** are at lower tier of instruction; errors begin to hinder comprehension; pronunciation may be influenced by native language; inconsistent use of basic-beginner structures (regular-verb endings, subject/verb/object word-order, plurals) as well as present/past/future.
	D	Below Target	**STUDENT SPEAKS BELOW INSTRUCTION LEVEL.** ☐ **SPEAKING** may not address task completely; sentences are often incomplete, repetitive, and disorganized; difficult to follow. ☐ **VOCABULARY** use is severely limited, often incorrect, and little current vocabulary is evident and/or incorrect. ☐ **STRUCTURES** are below level of instruction; errors make comprehension difficult; pronunciation is highly influenced by native language; incorrect use of basic-beginner structures far outweighs correct usage.
	F	Far-Below Target	**STUDENT SPEAKS FAR-BELOW INSTRUCTION LEVEL.** ☐ **SPEAKING** does not address task, sentences are incomplete; student made little attempt. ☐ **VOCABULARY** use is practically nonexistent, incorrect usage outweighs correct usage; little to no current vocabulary is evident and/or correct. ☐ **STRUCTURES** are far below level of instruction; errors predominate making comprehension extremely difficult, if not impossible; little evidence of correct usage.

Figure 2.10 Speaking Rubric

Class Chart

Make a ladder with 10 points on it (or more if you wish) and put it on a whiteboard or other board. During specified periods of time, ask students to speak only in the target language. If you hear anyone speaking in English, move a magnet on the chart from 10 points to 9. Each time someone speaks in English, the class loses a point. The class can earn points back if no one speaks any English for the entire length of the target-language speaking period. Decide how many points you will let them earn back. There are a variety of ways to track the points on the chart. One way is to use the points for a class participation grade. At the end of the week, whatever points are on the chart become a participation grade. A different option is to have students earn the points for a special party, video, or game day. Create some class competition by putting up three charts on the board. Divide the room and class in half. Monitor the use of the target language on the charts based on the sides of the room. Use the third chart to keep yourself in check. If the students catch you speaking in English without first asking permission, you lose points and they can earn one back. Use the charts for participation points or for incentives. The kids enjoy trying to catch you speaking in English!

Individual Charts

If the Class Chart system is ineffective in your classroom, consider creating a chart to track individual speaking points. This system will reflect individual rather than whole-class effort. Either track the number of times you hear the students speaking in the target language or track when you hear them speaking English. Tracking the number of times students speak in the target language can be a little more complicated. If you prefer to do that, consider using a seating chart. Indicate with a hash mark each time a student offers an answer in the target language. If you prefer to deduct points for speaking in English, try beginning the week with a specific amount of speaking points that students can keep by speaking only in the target language. Take a point away each time you hear the student speaking in English. See Figure 2.11 for a sample way to track the points you deduct. Simply cross out the points next to the student's name as he or she loses them. You may want to allow students to earn a point back if they go an entire class period without speaking English, especially as students get used to the system.

Capture the Flag Game

Brief Explanation

Begin each week by giving each student a flag of a country where your target language is spoken and ask the student to keep it on his or her desk in plain sight. The goal is for students to keep their individual flags until the end of the week, because that indicates they have spoken only the target language during the specified times in class. Students can lose their flags if they speak to the teacher or a classmate in English during a target language–only time frame. Indicate that it is a target language–only time period by posting a picture of a flag that represents a country that speaks your language. When English is acceptable, show the US flag. Any student hearing a classmate speaking in English should say in the target language, "You spoke in English. Give me your flag!" Make it clear that not speaking at all in Spanish during the course of the class period can cost them their flag if anyone catches them as well.

Additional Rules

To keep one's flag, the student must speak in the target language to at least three people during the course of the class period. You may also want to qualify that saying, "Hi," or something very simple does not count. Students can recapture a lost flag by catching another student speaking in English during the target language–only time

Use of Target Language Chart	Total	20	19	18	17	16	15	14	13	12	11	10	9	8	7	6	5	4	3	2	1
Anderson, Holly		20	19	18	17	16	15	14	13	12	11	10	9	8	7	6	5	4	3	2	1
Chamberlain, Oscar		20	19	18	17	16	15	14	13	12	11	10	9	8	7	6	5	4	3	2	1
Colby, Sara		20	19	18	17	16	15	14	13	12	11	10	9	8	7	6	5	4	3	2	1
Gray, Nicole		20	19	18	17	16	15	14	13	12	11	10	9	8	7	6	5	4	3	2	1
Hoffman, Jamie		20	19	18	17	16	15	14	13	12	11	10	9	8	7	6	5	4	3	2	1
Klopp, Sue		20	19	18	17	16	15	14	13	12	11	10	9	8	7	6	5	4	3	2	1
Kojis, Julie		20	19	18	17	16	15	14	13	12	11	10	9	8	7	6	5	4	3	2	1
Matt, Julie		20	19	18	17	16	15	14	13	12	11	10	9	8	7	6	5	4	3	2	1
Nies, Angela		20	19	18	17	16	15	14	13	12	11	10	9	8	7	6	5	4	3	2	1
Roberts, Mandy		20	19	18	17	16	15	14	13	12	11	10	9	8	7	6	5	4	3	2	1
Rosenberg, Amy		20	19	18	17	16	15	14	13	12	11	10	9	8	7	6	5	4	3	2	1
Schmidt, Mary		20	19	18	17	16	15	14	13	12	11	10	9	8	7	6	5	4	3	2	1
Tallon, Jim		20	19	18	17	16	15	14	13	12	11	10	9	8	7	6	5	4	3	2	1
Taylor, Stephanie		20	19	18	17	16	15	14	13	12	11	10	9	8	7	6	5	4	3	2	1
Zimmer, Tim		20	19	18	17	16	15	14	13	12	11	10	9	8	7	6	5	4	3	2	1

Figure 2.11 Use of Target Language Chart

Note: This is a sample. The downloadable version is blank for your own use.

period. Students can acquire more than one flag. Those who do so are eligible for a prize, extra participation points, or whatever you would like to offer at the end of each week. Also tell students who acquire additional flags that they may not just give an extra flag to another student at the end of the week. Students may not attempt to steal another student's flag by removing it from their desk or personal belongings. Students may never speak to you in English without first asking for permission, unless you have a picture of the flag of the United States showing on the board. If the students speak to you in English, they must turn their flags over to you and won't have the chance to get them back until the following week.

Ways for Students to Get Their Flags Back

If you want to provide students with a chance to get their flags back in a way other than having to catch another student speaking English, offer them a chance to *duel* with another student who has two or more flags. During a time acceptable to the teacher, the student challenger says to the other student, "I challenge you to a flag duel!" Although it sounds a little corny, the students do like to challenge each other! The student who was challenged must accept, and the two stand in front of the class. The challenger must have three questions prepared (and memorized) for the other student in the target language that would be considered *fair game* because they have been previously taught or are in the current lesson. The challenger can ask up to three questions. If the challenged student cannot answer all three, the challenged must surrender the extra flag and the duel is over. Only students with two or more flags can be challenged to duels. Any student can challenge another to a duel, but a losing challenger also loses a flag. The duels are great because they are a way to keep kids on top of any essential questions you have given them and they challenge students to form more complex questions to stump their opponent.

Tips for Making the Flags

Print the flags on cardstock and laminate them if you would like to reuse them every week. Printing the flags in color is a benefit as well if you have access to a color printer. If you want to reinforce geography, label the country and its capital on the cardstock just above the flag. Make yourself a flag of the United States and one of a country that represents your language. Paste the flags back-to-back on a piece of construction paper and laminate. If you have a magnetized whiteboard, get a magnet clip and clip your flag to the board where all the students can see it. Indicate what language to speak by flipping the flag to the appropriate side.

3

Warm-Up Activities

Activity & Brief Description	Page	Application Areas				Type of Communication	
		VO	GR	CO	CU	Oral	Written
Conversation of the Day Provide a topic and ask students to have a quick conversation about it.	36	•	•	•	•	•	
Daily News Ask students to report on things they did, are doing, or will be doing.	36	•	•	•		•	
Current Events Students make a brief presentation about something important occurring in the world.	37	•	•	•	•	•	•
Expression of the Day/Week Provide students with an important expression each day.	37	•	•	•	•	•	•
Questions of the Day Students answer questions in a variety of ways from text, visuals, or audio.	38	•	•	•	•	•	•
Report of the Day	38	•	•	•	•	•	•
Special People	39	•	•			•	•
VO = Vocabulary	GR = Grammar			CO = Content			CU = Culture

This chapter highlights activities you can do to begin your class. The activities are intended to provide a variety of options to keep warm-up activities fresh. Some of the activities, like the Report of the Day, can easily be done in conjunction with another warm-up activity. These activities can be written on whiteboards or on paper in a notebook so students can see a record of their work. The daily warm-up can also be written on a sheet that you collect periodically with space for multiple days' worth of warm-ups or on a quarter-sheet of paper. You can collect the quarter-sheet of paper daily or frequently so you can have concrete samples of student work and see more closely the areas in which they may be struggling. While the activities are explained as warm-ups, they really could be adapted to work at any point of the class, or even to give you information on an exit ticket.

Conversation of the Day

Objectives: Speak about a topic of importance to the lesson or students' daily lives.

Materials: Materials vary by topic; some possibilities are as follows:

- ° Key questions list

- ° A section of a dialogue

- ° Quick Chat card

- ° Role-play card

Activity Directions and Preparation Hints

Begin class by having students converse about a topic you predetermine. Here are some possible ideas:

- A review of essential questions from the current or a previous chapter

- A prompt from a Quick Chat card

- A couple of questions that later form part of a dialogue you want the students to memorize

- A mini–role-play situation

- A cartoon to interpret

- A statement or text to debate

- An image, cultural if possible, for students to describe or discuss, or to prompt a conversation that could take place at the location of the image

- A persuasive conversation or debate with a visual and/or textual prompt

   - ° Show two different competing products. Each student takes the job of trying to convince the other why they should buy "their" product.

      - – Two movie posters, book covers, cars, etc.

Ask students to speak only in the target language during this time period. After the student practice period ends, call on a few students in the class to answer the essential questions they focused on, have the conversation, or do the role-play. A few minutes of oral practice a day goes a long way in improving the student's speaking skills.

Daily News

Objectives: Share events that happened or are going to happen.

Materials: Reference sheets with commonly stated phrases in the past and future tenses

Activity Directions and Preparation Hints

Choose a specific day or days when students share things that they are going to do or already did. This is a great way to practice the future and past tenses before and after they have been formally introduced in class. Provide students with an example sheet of things they might be apt to say, so they have various models of how to form conjugations with each of the different types of verb endings. Also provide them with examples of irregular high-frequency verbs. Fridays are good days to have students talk about what they are going to do over the weekend, and Mondays are great for having students share what they did over the weekend. You may want to have them begin by telling their partners three things they did. Then ask for volunteers to share with the class. Some teachers use this as an announcements activity where students need to prepare something to share with the class and they stand up in front to do so. If you have students do announcements, you may want to engage the rest of the class more by having them jot down the key information they heard from the speaker.

Applications and Modifications

Using this same idea, once students are comfortable with answering questions in the first-person singular, you can begin to introduce other forms and have the students ask each other questions. Then students can share with the class what their partner is going to do or did, or talk about something they both did, and so forth.

Current Events

Objectives: Identify important events occurring in the countries you teach about.

Materials: Articles students find with current events

Activity Directions and Preparation Hints

Have students bring in and share current events happening in the countries that speak your target language. Students can find an article independently or as a pair. One way to do this is by having students create comprehension questions for the class, either in English or the target language. Students finding the article should send you the link and the comprehension questions prior to the day they will present so you can assign the article and questions to the rest of the class as homework to prepare. On the day the homework is due, the students will lead the discussion. The discussion can be whole-class or start with pairs and then lead into a whole-group discussion. You can designate a day that current events will be shared and then have students sign up at the beginning of the semester for their week.

Expression of the Day/Week

Objectives: Learn expressions to improve students' base of spoken phrases.

Materials: List of important classroom expressions

Activity Directions and Preparation Hints

Using the list of important expressions for your class, write the phrase of the day or week in an identified location on the board or post it on a bulletin board. Also add the expressions to a stack of flashcards to review as a class and/or put them in a presentation file to show the meaning visually with the text whenever possible. Pronounce the expression and use it in context. Explain any differences in literal and actual meaning. Pick sayings, idiomatic expressions, daily use questions or phrases, appropriate slang words they would want to know, or other helpful expressions. Challenge students to use them accurately in context, when speaking with a partner or writing at some point during the hour each day.

Questions of the Day

Objectives: Practice asking and answering questions in written and oral forms.

Materials: Questions projected or written on the board

Questions of the day serve as a warm-up activity for students to practice any content, culture, vocabulary, or grammar that you would like and at the same time reinforce how to ask and answer questions. Depending upon how much time you want to take to do them and the facility with which your students answer questions, you may want to stick to 3–5 questions. Once students have written their answers, you can discuss them as a class first or have students discuss the answers to their questions with one another. This activity can help students who are less confident speaking, as they will have their answers to reference. The questions of the day can come with a visual about which to write a response or responses, which can also help spark the conversation. To vary the questions for the students, you could create a sequence something like this:

Monday: Students respond in writing to written questions on the board with or without a visual aid.

Tuesday: Students respond in written form to questions that are read to them orally.

Wednesday: Students listen to an audio clip (song, commercial, video clip, content-based audio, etc.) and answer questions about it.

Thursday: Students write the questions that go with provided answers.

Friday: Students play the 20 Questions game, where students try to guess the information that only you or another student knows by asking yes or no questions.

On all days except Friday, students could still discuss the questions and answers with a partner after the written or listening part of the activity.

Report of the Day

Objectives: Review important topics relevant to daily routine.

Materials: Questions projected or written on the board

The Daily Report works well with things students would want to know or plan for on a daily basis and helps to review topics in a context on a daily or regular basis. It is helpful as over time students will learn the topics you choose and you can save yourself from having to do entire units on them. You can do related activities to reinforce them, but shouldn't need a whole unit. Some topics that work well for the Daily Report are: telling the day, date, weather, and the time of an event or class. Other topics that work well are clothing you will need to wear that morning, afternoon, or evening, recommended activities on what to do after school based on the weather or season, what you are going to do after school, and what you ate for breakfast or lunch or will eat for dinner. You will likely want to make a page in presentation software like Google Presentation, PowerPoint, Keynote, or Open Office, as you will use it regularly. You can also integrate quick weather reports in your target language and then also include geography by showing where the country is on a map, give news about activities when talking about the recommended activities, talk about the time and any differences there may be with use of the 24-hour clock, and more.

Special People

Objectives: Review important topics relevant to daily routine.

Materials: Questions projected or written on the board

This activity is a whole-group questioning activity adapted from ideas from Bryce Hedstrom. The teacher or the students and teacher determine a set of questions that they are going to use to learn more about the students in the class. The questions should provide students with opportunities to develop their abilities to ask and answer questions about common conversational topics, topics that support your curricular goals, and/or topics of special interest to the students. Each day you can interview 2–4 students, on average, depending upon the interest level of the students and how long each interview lasts. It is helpful to have a sheet of paper with a table in it (Figure 3.1) so you and your students can record the information about their classmates. You may also have students just take notes in a notebook. Going through students in alphabetical order may be helpful in locating notes for future use.

It is also very helpful for you and students to have a presentation that has the key questions and answer structures, as well as any other relevant information they would need that they would not already know in order to answer the questions. For the example, part of the purpose is to practice numbers 1–31, months, and date formation, so a page that lays all of that information out for students to see how to spell the numbers and months is extremely useful. It is also helpful for teaching additional vocabulary. One example of that is when talking about family, particularly siblings. While the primary purpose may be to find out the number and names of siblings, you can extend the conversation easily and incidentally teach other terms, like older, younger, works, high school, elementary school, etc., by having those words on the screen and asking more questions about their siblings.

Since students will hear the question as many times as there are students in the class, it is a nice way to reinforce important questions and their answer structure. After you interview the students for the day, give students another opportunity to learn about their classmates by asking them varied comprehension questions. Who has a birthday in summer? Who was born in a southern state? Who is the oldest student in the class so far? Who has the closest birthday to Day of the Dead? You may want to periodically give an open notes "quiz" on the information. It could count for a homework grade or small quiz. You will want to keep the quiz general so you can use it with more than one class, unless you want to make a separate quiz for each. You may also want to make one slide with all of the questions in your target language for students to ask one another before or after the day's interviews. This way they can also engage in oral practice. You can take it a step further by providing another slide that has bulleted questions/topics to discuss in English so they will need to think of the target language questions independently. This can give you formative assessment data and can also serve as a prompt for a summative oral assessment at the end of the interview cycle.

The information from your interviews can also be used for other class activities or for guessing games when students don't have their notes out. You could also graph data from the student information, compare and contrast, map people's birthplaces, and much more. This activity can be repeated throughout the year, based on time and student interest. It does not have to be done every day, but it can be part of your daily routine and provides a way to continually learn about your students through the target language.

Name	Birthday	Age	City you are from	Favorite book/ movie
Self				
1.				
2.				
3.				
4.				
5.				
6.				
7.				
8.				
9.				
10.				

Figure 3.1 Special People Table

4

Individual Practice Activities

Activity & Brief Description	Page	Application Areas				Type of Communication	
		VO	GR	CO	CU	Oral	Written
Apps and Websites Students use websites and apps to learn independently in class and beyond.	42	•	•				•
Actions Students stand up and do the actions that correspond to the commands given by you to show comprehension.	43	•	•				
Interactive Objects Students hold up pictures of the vocabulary they are learning to indicate their comprehension of the word.	43	•	•	•	•	•	•
Journal Writing Students keep a journal in the target language. Use it to do impromptu writing in class and for writing assignments to be completed at home.	44	•	•	•	•		•
Mad Libs Students receive a sheet with various parts of speech used to complete a usually humorous story. The student fills in a word that fits and then transfers it to the blanks in the story.	45	•	•	•	•	•	•
Songs Students participate in song activities that support a particular content, culture, grammar, or vocabulary topic.	46	•	•	•	•	•	•
Worksheets Students complete worksheets that allow you to assess their comprehension of a topic.	47	•	•	•	•		•

VO = Vocabulary GR = Grammar CO = Content CU = Culture

Individual Practice Activities

Apps and Websites

Objectives: Provide students with tools to use on school or their own personal devices that allow them to progress at their own speed; help students find tools that work well for them as learners.

Materials: Any device that can access the Internet (apps will require access for the initial download or for information updates)

If your technology situation at school allows it, providing time for individual practice provides students with an opportunity to progress independently and at their own pace. There are too many websites and apps to catalogue that have great resources for student learning. To keep up with those, becoming part of a professional learning network (PLN) online will be valuable. Following #langchat, #actfl, #csctfl, #edchat, #fliplang, #sk12, or #mlearning on Twitter can help you connect with other teachers who are part of an online community of learners. It is also helpful for finding new resources, staying current, and dialoguing with other educators. Another place to build your PLN is Facebook, by following the posts of your state's world language organization, as well as others, such as: www.actfl.org, www.iallt.org, www.waflt.org, and https://calico.org.

Become familiar with apps that students can use independently at school or at home to extend their learning to be anywhere and anytime. You can take some time to look around in the Apple App Store as well as in Google Play to see what is available in your language. Don't forget to look for apps that students can use to create. For Apple devices, Voice Record easily makes and shares voice recordings. Shadow Puppet Edu allows students to access images within the app to make presentations with text and voice. Pic Collage allows students to make collages that could be used for storytelling, explaining a process, and more. Other educators have also taken the time to catalogue good apps and blog about them. One such blog that offers many useful resources for technology and learning is http://larryferlazzo. edublogs.org/. Another great blog to follow for technology in general is Richard Byrne's www.freetech4teachers.com. I have also found blog sites to follow on Pinterest. The trick is to just pick a few to read so you don't become overwhelmed. You can also subscribe to the blogs so you will get automatic emails when there is a new post.

The following sites/apps were chosen because of their quality, accessibility, engaging nature, and facility with which students can make progress at their own pace. They are web-based and have apps for Apple and Android devices. At the time of this edition, they are all free!

Duolingo

Duolingo (www.duolingo.com) is a free language learning site that provides a course path that students work through at their own speed. They complete modules and engage with visual, audio, and translation activities. Students are provided with words to choose from in beginning stages of learning new topics and are supported with grammatical explanations and definitions as needed. Students can earn Lingots and follow and compete with friends. Students can also duel with a classmate or a Duolingo Bot to sharpen their skills. Additionally, students can do real-world practice by helping to translate texts uploaded to the site. More languages continue to be developed, but currently English speakers can learn Spanish, French, German, Italian, and Portuguese.

Memrise

If you would like to access existing material or generate your own vocabulary content, you may also want to consider Memrise (www.memrise.com). Users can search for existing courses in a variety of languages or create their own course to match their own course content. Memrise uses the premise of a garden, so students are planting when

Individual Practice Activities

learning new material and watering when reviewing. Memrise uses a combination of user-recorded and existing audio. Users (teachers or students) can create Mems, which are visuals that use a mnemonic phrase with a visual to help users visualize. Users are asked a variety of questions that get progressively more difficult once they have initially practiced. At first users are introduced to about three words at a time, which users practice in various ways before new ones are added. Users can easily create and move around different levels. Language flashcards can go from English to the target language or target language to target language. You just need to put the target language clue in where it says English. A multimedia level is also available for YouTube videos or presentations in a resource like SlideShare. This could be valuable for students wanting to work at their own pace or wanting a review before beginning the next level. I can see this working nicely for practicing song vocabulary as well. Students could practice vocabulary and then watch a music video as part of the learning sequence. This could also be a nice resource for students to use for review over the summer. See the Resources and References section of the book for additional recommended sites.

Actions

Objectives: Do actions to aid in vocabulary recall.

Materials: None

Activity Directions and Preparation Hints

Whenever possible, teach vocabulary words with an action. Use Total Physical Response to get students out of their desks and doing the movement for the word as they hear it. Actions lend themselves particularly well to teaching tangible verbs and nouns.

Examples of Total Physical Response are as follows:

- *Run*: Ask students to run in place.

- *Ran*: Have students run in place, and point behind their shoulders with their thumb to illustrate that the action happened in the past.

- *I am hungry*: Students rub their stomachs and show an expression of hunger on their faces.

- *How gross!*: Students make a disgusted face.

- *Tricycle*: Students pretend to ride a tricycle.

- *Couch*: Students pretend to lie back on the couch and flip through the television channels with an imaginary remote.

Interactive Objects

Objectives: Use manipulatives to practice vocabulary.

Materials: Pictures of the objects you are going to teach

Activity Directions and Preparation Hints

Make copies of the objects you want to teach. For a unit on clothing, find visual aids of the different clothing items you would like students to learn. Copy them onto cardstock. Cut them out yourself and put a set into an envelope for each student, or have the students cut them out before the activity starts. Ask students to hold them up as you say the name of them. Ask for student volunteers to state an object for the class to hold up.

Applications and Modifications

Modification 1: Pair Practice

Materials: Object flashcards

Have the students work in pairs to practice the new vocabulary words. Make sure that they both have a vocabulary list to use as reference if they need it. One student should have the vocabulary list, and ask the other to hold up the correct object. The student can make the task more challenging by holding up the object and asking their partner to say its name in the target language. Ask students to take turns with each role.

Modification 2: The Flyswatter Game

Materials: Object flashcards

Have students play the Flyswatter Game using the cut-out pictures. As you call out the name of the object, the first student to pick up the correct object gets the point. Modify this by having students form a group of three. One student calls out the word while the other two play. Students can play more than one round.

Modification 3: Writing Practice

Materials: Object flashcards, blank sheet of paper

Have students pick six to eight object flashcards and write sentences or questions that include those words. Or ask students to use them in a dialogue, paragraph, or short story. If students write questions, they also can be used for oral or written question and answer practice with a partner.

Journal Writing

Objectives: Use vocabulary to express ideas in writing.

Materials: Blank sheet of paper, notebook or blog site

Activity Directions and Preparation Hints

An excellent way for students to use the vocabulary they learn is by applying it in journal writing. Determine how many times you would like them to write and how to assess it. Communicate with your language arts teachers to see how you can mutually support one another's writing goals by using common language and to inquire about what types of reading and writing they are doing. Choose topics that support your units, as well as topics that interest your students. Journal writing does not have to create an excessive amount of correcting for you. Decide which journals you will read just for content and which you will correct for grammar and vocabulary errors. What students find the most valuable for their improvement is constructive feedback and guidance. Avoid feeling like you have to grade everything that they write. Consider a rotation for grading so once every 2–3 weeks students get thoughtful oral or written feedback from you.

Many students and teachers enjoy utilizing a blog for writing. Blogs offer a chronological order in which to organize student work and a way for students and teachers to access writing from home without needing notebooks. Blogs offer an opportunity for students to see the work of their peers to get ideas on improving their own work, to comment on the thoughts expressed by their peers, to give constructive feedback, to have an audience beyond the teacher for their work, and to keep work neatly organized. Talk to your students and determine which tool is the best for you and for them, based on the resources you have available and the preferences of your students. You may even allow some to use a notebook, while others post on the blog. A few blog sites you may want to take a look at include: www.kidblog.org, www.teacherblogit.com, and www.edublogs.org. Teacher Blog It is completely free, and the other two have limited free options. Each of the sites offers different features, but most also allow the posting of videos and images, which can add more meaning to the textual part of the blog.

Mad Libs

Objectives: Recall parts of speech and identify vocabulary to fit in various categories of speech.

Materials: Mad Libs worksheets

Activity Directions and Preparation Hints

Mad Libs help students practice parts of speech in a humorous way. You can purchase ready-made Mad Libs or create your own. Two parts are involved in creating Mad Libs. First, find or write a paragraph related to the teaching objective. Try to set up the Mad Libs so the paragraph turns out to be funny or somewhat bizarre. Then decide what parts of speech you want to highlight.

Next, remove 15 to 20 words from the paragraph you wrote or found, making a cloze activity. Replace the word with a line, and write the number below the line to correspond to a separate worksheet. On the separate worksheet, number it and include blanks to correspond to the numbered blanks of the cloze paragraph. Below each line write in the corresponding part of speech for the missing word. For each number on the worksheet, the student must fill in a word that fits the indicated part of speech, such as a third-person singular verb, a noun to describe a politician, a large number, a place, and so forth.

When students do the activity, first pass out the worksheet and have the students fill it in. Afterward, pass out the paragraph cloze activity and have the students transfer their words to it. Then, have them read the paragraph and see how strange or funny it turns out. As an extension, have the student write comprehension questions to go with their new story, in the format of true/false, logical/illogical, multiple choice, or short answer. You could differentiate by having stronger students take on more challenging comprehension question tasks.

Applications and Modifications

Mad Libs have various extensions and are great for practicing the parts of speech. Ask your students to read their Mad Lib aloud to their partner and decide which is funnier. You can also ask them to answer comprehension questions about their Mad Lib. Ask students to write their own Mad Lib or a sequel to yours.

Application 1: Cultural and Content-Based Mad Libs

Materials: Mad Libs worksheets

Find or write a Mad Lib based on a cultural topic or historical figure. Try using a famous poem or excerpt from a novel your students are reading and strategically remove words for a new twist on the selection. After students have filled in the paragraph with their bizarre answers, discuss what changes would be necessary to make the paragraph true.

Sample Topics:

- Noun-adjective order modeling

- Noun-adjective agreement in gender and number

- Subject-verb agreement

- Any vocabulary you would like to review

- Cultural topics such as festivals, artists, historical figures, and so forth

- Content-based vocabulary

Songs

Objectives: Learn and recall vocabulary and grammatical topics.

Materials: Songs in the target language

Activity Directions and Preparation Hints

Use songs to teach vocabulary and grammar whenever possible. Songs are one of the most powerful teaching tools because once we learn them, we tend not to forget them. Think about all the song lyrics you have stored in your own head and how many songs you can easily sing along with. Any money spent on good songs in the world language is well worth it. Make sure to check www.youtube.com to find authentic music, like children's songs and popular music, songs created to teach vocabulary and grammar to non-native speakers, and interviews with or about musicians. You can also look for videos about the style of the music and for videos that teach the dance steps or moves to the song, if there are any. Look for the original music videos, karaoke versions, student- or teacher-made music videos, and other versions of the song made by others that tell the story of the song through pictures and subtitles. You can also search for behind the scenes videos that show and explain the making of the music videos. Searching for the song and lyrics is helpful for singing along. If you have props that go well with the song, make sure to pull those out too!

Application 1: Song Listening Activities

Materials: Song audio (and video if available), song activity

Use songs by popular artists as sources for listening activities. To get started, do a lyrics search on the Internet. Make sure to check them for correct spelling and accents because oftentimes they do have some errors. Do your best to find a song that has some words or grammatical structures your students recognize. It's even better if you can find something that reinforces a current or recent area of study. Save the lyrics in a word processing document. Once you have saved a master with all the lyrics, turn the song into a cloze activity by removing select words and replacing them with a blank for students to fill in as they listen to the song. One approach is to leave multiple blanks for students to fill in. You can also select just a few words for students to fill in, using the song as a way to teach or reinforce those particular words. A combined approach would be to select words that students should already know and 3–4 new ones that you want them to learn. Depending on the level of your students, provide them with a word bank. You can also just provide a word bank for words that are new to them and have them work to recognize the familiar ones without the bank. Once students have had a few opportunities to listen to the song, go over the answers with them. You may want to play the song once each day at the beginning of class until they have had ample opportunities to fill in the blanks.

Decide if you would like to do a follow-up activity. Here are some options:

- Having students sing along for a period of time at the beginning of each hour

- Putting on a lip sync contest

- Dividing the song up and assigning students in groups to translate a part of the song

- Having students highlight a grammatical feature they have been practicing

- Asking students to research the artist of the song

- Having students follow the artist on Twitter for a month or more and then report back on their tweets

- Discussing the song in pairs or small groups, allowing them to share opinions, discuss and clarify meaning, write a new or alternate verse for the song, etc.

- Writing and sending an email or tweet to the singer and/or songwriter of the song

- Learning the song and performing it for the class (vocal and/or instrumental)

- Teaching the steps to the music if there are any (use a video from YouTube or another source if you do not feel confident)

An extensive resource for using songs in the classroom is *You Played a Song, Now What?* by Sue Fenton (2003). Zachary Jones has a helpful website called Zambombazo: http://zachary-jones.com/zambombazo, which can be referenced for activities and ideas for using songs. While it is for Spanish music, other language teachers may also like it for the ideas it has.

Worksheets

Objectives: Practice and recall any topic.

Materials: Worksheets

Activity Directions and Preparation Hints

Although you don't want to overuse worksheets, they are useful tools provided the tasks students are being asked to do are meaningful. Use them for homework and occasional practice in class. A worksheet written with a purpose other than to fill time can be a good tool to quickly determine whether your students comprehend something you taught. While they work on it, circulate through the room and check to see if students seem to understand the concept. Offer constructive feedback when needed. Students tend to ask you more questions about their work when you circulate through the room.

Pair Activities

Activity & Brief Description	Page	Application Areas				Type of Communication	
		VO	GR	CO	CU	Oral	Written
Back-to-Back Write questions in the first column of a two-column table. Write the answers on index cards. Each student sticks the card on his or her back. Students move around and find the answer to their question from the cards and record them in the second column of their sheet.	51	•	•	•	•	•	•
Blindfold Course Each student takes a turn walking a blindfolded partner through the school, giving directions in the target language about where to turn.	52	•	•			•	
Dice Games With two different colors of dice, one representing subjects and the other verbs, create six different topics and six different verbs to correspond to a number 1–6 for each side of the die. Students roll and conjugate the verb. Students can also use a third die to form sentences. There are various review options with this game.	52	•	•	•	•	•	•
Eyewitness Reports One student interviews another to get an account of an event.	54	•	•	•	•	•	•
Find the Errors First! Students work in pairs or against one another to identify all of the errors in a passage.	56	•	•	•	•	•	•
Get Around It This is a circumlocution activity. Students take turns describing a word to a partner without saying the word itself. The partner must guess the word.	57	•	•	•		•	•

Activity & Brief Description	Page	Application Areas				Type of Communication	
		VO	GR	CO	CU	Oral	Written
Happily Ever After? Students work together, using the target language to write an alternative ending or a sequel to a well-known fairy tale or poem.	58	•	•		•		•
Hear/Say Activities Give students a sheet with two columns. One column has a word students say and the other they hear. Students take turns listening so they can find the match to what they heard in the listening column. They then look across to the speaking column and say the word listed there. Students keep the sequence going until the end.	59	•	•	•	•	•	•
Imaginary Room Students make a list of items they have in their imaginary room (or other enclosed space). Each student tries to guess his or her partner's objects.	61	•	•	•	•		•
Information Gap Activities Although there are many variations of these activities, the premise is that one student collects information from another that he or she needs to complete a task or activity.	62	•	•	•	•	•	•
Off the Top of My Head . . . Ask students to write down the first four words that come to their minds, ensuring they have a least one verb, noun, and adjective. Students then circulate and record all the words from six other students. When students finish, they write a piece that includes all the words they collected.	64					•	•
Or Students have a list of choices (dog or cat, ice cream or cake, etc.). They discuss why they like one over the other.	64	•	•	•	•	•	•
Order It! Give students 8–12 slips of paper, each with a sentence on it. Their task is to put the sentences in a logical order.	65	•	•	•	•	•	•

Pair Activities

Activity & Brief Description	Page	Application Areas				Type of Communication	
		VO	GR	CO	CU	Oral	Written
Partner Interview and Challenge Students interview each other with a teacher-provided questionnaire and record the answers. Students then turn over their papers. The teacher proceeds to ask the pairs the same questions they asked their partner, except now the students must remember and write down their partner's answers.	67	•	•			•	•
Roll for It! Divide the class into pairs. Students answer a question from you on their whiteboards. The first student to answer correctly rolls the dice for points. Students keep track of their points, and the one with the most at the end of the game wins.	68	•	•	•	•		•
Sentence Scramble Students receive words in an envelope. They need to make as many logical sentences as they can, using only the words they have.	69	•	•	•			•
Silly Sentences Give students a sheet with 10–12 sentences on it. Some of them should be logical and others silly. Students must identify which are logical and which are not.	71	•	•			•	•
Simple Pair Activities Students take turns quizzing each other with pictures, gestures, or word lists.	72	•	•	•	•	•	•
That's Odd! Students are given a sheet with sets of four-word combinations. Students must determine which word does not fit in the group and write a response in the target language, explaining why it does not fit.	74	•	•	•	•	•	•
Where Is It? Give each student in the pair a drawing of a house or some other drawing with multiple sections or rooms. Students put up a folder between them as a barrier and hide an object somewhere in their diagram. Both students must ask questions to guess where their partner's object is.	74	•	•			•	•

VO = Vocabulary GR = Grammar CO = Content CU = Culture

Pair Activities

Back-to-Back

Objectives: Find the correct response to a question.

Materials: Back-to-back worksheet, tape

Activity Directions and Preparation Hints

Students can practice vocabulary, grammar, content, and culture in the Back-to-Back activity. Use it to review essential information for a quiz. Once students complete the activity, they have a review sheet with the most important information they need to look over again at home.

Here is an example of one way to do this for a vocabulary quiz. Prepare a sheet with vocabulary pictures that you would like students to identify in the target language. Pass them out and have each student stick a sheet to their back. They need to move around the room and get other people to write in one answer until they fill up their sheet. Each student should remove the sheet and check and correct it for spelling errors, using the master vocabulary sheet. Make it a competition by having the first student who has no spelling errors on the sheet come to you with the sheet and get a prize if it is completely correct.

Applications and Modification

Modification 1: Find the Answers

Materials: Back-to-Back worksheet, set of index cards with answers

Prepare a sheet with questions to which you would like students to find an answer. Also, prepare a set of index cards that have the answers to your questions. Tape an answer card on each student's back. Have the students walk around the classroom to find the answer to their questions. The questions should seek some sort of information that students wouldn't be able to answer easily without the card. Also, they need to know that there is only one answer, so they cannot invent any of their own answers for this one. If possible, use names of students in your class when asking questions about people. If you create the question and answer set in Quizlet, you can print it out from there. You can also use the Quizlet set for small or whole group practice as well.

Sample Questions:

- Where is the bank?

- Why didn't Sara go to school yesterday?

- How much candy did Steve buy on Friday?

- Who is playing basketball in the gym?

Sample Topics:

- Any vocabulary word or phrase

- Essential questions you need to know when on vacation

- Answering questions in the first person of the past tense

Blindfold Course

Objectives: Use vocabulary for giving directions.

Materials: Enough bandanas for half of your students

Activity Directions and Preparation Hints

This activity works well for practicing directions and places in the school. It could be a good way for new students to get to know their way around the building better as well. It also works nicely as a trust-building activity. Divide students into pairs. Give the first student in the pair a map of the inside of the school building, showing a path along which they must lead their partner. Have a couple of different maps drawn up so students don't all go off in the same direction. Leaders must blindfold their partners and take them on the path, starting at your classroom door, giving them directions in the target language, and making sure they stay out of danger. The blindfolded partner evaluates how well his or her partner communicated. Students may not speak to each other in English. If anyone hears them, they are disqualified and do not receive points for the activity. The partners then switch roles. The new leader should not use the same path his or her partner took.

Dice Games

Objectives: Conjugate verbs and form complete sentences.

Materials: Dice game worksheet, set of three dice in different colors for each pair of students

Activity Directions and Preparation Hints

You need three sets of dice, each a different color, to play the dice game. You also need a worksheet with three numbered lists divided into three columns of categories: subjects, verbs in their infinitive form, and nouns (Figure 5.1). Include six items per category, assigning each item to one number in your list. At the top of each column, write the color of one of the dice that you have. Students working in pairs roll the three dice and match the number on the die with the number and word in each corresponding column to form a sentence. Students can be asked to form the sentence orally or write it down. It is more challenging if you mix nouns and verbs that do not make logical sentences. When writing the sentences, students should be asked to determine if they make sense. If they don't, they should not write them down on their worksheet. This is one way you can check to see if the students comprehend the meanings of their sentences. If you have an interactive whiteboard, check your tools to see if you have interactive dice. If you do, you can easily model the activity, play it as a whole class, or create a station activity for students.

Applications and Modification

Modification 1: Verbs in Chart Already Conjugated

Materials: Dice game worksheet, sets of three dice in different colors for each pair of students

Here is a modification for if you are just beginning to teach verb conjugations. Put the subject pronoun in the first column, one verb in its conjugated forms in the second column, and an object in the third column. Check to see

Pair Activities

A. Conjugate the model verb in the chart.

Target Language Verb	Definition
I	we
you	you all
he, she, you formal, it	they, you all

B. Pick up red, green, and white dice. Roll them to make a sentence.

Red	Green	White
1. I	1. to eat	1. the white shoes
2. you	2. to buy	2. the gigantic cookie
3. she	3. to wear	3. the green frog
4. we	4. to look for	4. the pink house
5. you all	5. to drink	5. the lemonade
6. they	6. to dance	6. the new book

C. Write down the sentences that you made by rolling the dice, but only if they make sense!

1. _____

2. _____

3. _____

4. _____

5. _____

6. _____

7. _____

8. _____

9. _____

10. _____

Figure 5.1 The Dice Game

if students can correctly match the conjugated verb to its subject. Tell them they can write a sentence only if the subject and verb agree. Use this modification with the verb *to be* and put adjectives in the third column to practice agreement.

Writing Extension: One extension for this activity is to have students try to write a short narrative that includes most or all of the sentences they made during the activity.

Sample Topics:

- Subject-verb agreement for any tense

- Logical sentence formation

- Noun-adjective agreement

- Subjects and predicates

- *Ser* versus *estar* (two verbs that both mean to be in Spanish) and a correct matching adjective

Eyewitness Reports

Objectives: Conduct an interview to collect information about a situation that occurred.

Materials: Incident record sheet

Activity Directions and Preparation Hints

In this activity students interview one another about an event to collect the details of the situation. Students take turns being the interviewer and the interviewee. If you have a recording device, have students record their interview so they can play back the conversation and self- or peer-evaluate their fluency, pronunciation, grammar, or other area. You can also have them turn it in to you. Use this activity to practice vocabulary related to a particular topic and relevant grammatical structures. With novice students, provide them with a fact sheet of what happened to help them answer their partner's questions. You can also create a mock-up picture of the suspect. You could easily search out some fun images online or have students bring in some that you can choose from. You can hand out a picture to each interviewee for the activity. You may want to pass around 4–6 different ones. That way at the end students could have to guess which one it was from the 4–6 that you project on the board after the activity. This would allow you to bring everyone back after their activities to discuss. You can also then as a follow-up homework ask students to take the information from their incident form and write it up into a formal police report.

For students with more vocabulary, provide them with additional things they need to include in the report that all students get to fill out (Figure 5.2). That might include the kind of incident and other information that connects to your unit of study. Encourage students to have creative, unlikely, or unexpected things happen in their accounts to make their retellings of the incident more entertaining. To save time you may also want to have students submit ideas, providing them with a couple of examples like those listed in the following sample reports to get them thinking creatively. You could then select one for the whole class to use or offer some options.

Date of incident: _____

Time of incident: _____

Place of incident: _____

Description of Suspect

Approximate age of suspect: _____

Eye color: _____ Hair color: _____

Approximate height: _____ Approximate weight: _____

Distinguishing features: _____

Clothing he/she was wearing: _____

_____

Description of any vehicles involved: _____

Description of incident (be as detailed as possible):

_____

_____

_____

_____

_____

_____

Reporter's Contact Information

Name of person reporting incident: _____

Address: _____

Phone number: _____

Cell phone number: _____

Best time to contact: _____

Figure 5.2 Incident Report Record

Applications and Modifications

Modification 1: UFO sighting

Materials: Incident fact sheet, incident record sheet

Make a witness statement report for a UFO sighting. Some information you might include in the report is the following: time; date; location; description of the ship; description of the aliens, including if they have hair, number of eyes, ears, arms, and legs; color of the alien; any personality traits determined from their actions or behaviors; whether they tried to communicate and the language they spoke; and so forth. The interviewer should also take down the contact information for the person interviewed, including name of witness, address, email address, and phone numbers (home and cell). The students can make up fictitious addresses and phone numbers if they do not want to use their real ones. Ask the student interviewer to write a summary of the incident's events in a paragraph and draw a sketch of the alien and its ship as well.

The following are a selection of other ideas for reports:

- Hollywood star sighting in Eagle River, Wisconsin

- Tornado sighting by a tornado chaser in Texas

- Hospital admissions report for someone who got hit on the head by plates that flew off a shelf during an earthquake

- Hurricane survivor's report

- Auto accident report because a turkey flew into the windshield

- Police report for theft of the family poodle, Princess

Find the Errors First!

Objectives: Apply grammar rules to find errors in written statements.

Materials: One or two lists of sentences with errors in them

Activity Directions and Preparation Hints

This game has multiple uses because it can be applied to any grammatical, vocabulary, historical, or cultural topic. Give the students a list of sentences in which there are a predetermined number of errors. The challenge is to see who can find and correct the most errors first. Make the task easier by indicating the number of errors at the end of each sentence. Play the game where one pair challenges another or as a partner challenge where each student gets the same list and competes against a partner.

Applications and Modifications

Modification 1: Two-Team Class Competition

Materials: A projected or paper copy list of sentences with errors in them, whiteboards, dry-erase markers

Prepare sentences to project that have errors and pass out whiteboards to all students. Divide the class into two teams. Show the first sentence with errors in it, and tell students they need to rewrite the sentence, correcting all the errors. Each person on the team is responsible for writing down the corrected sentence. Teammates then compare and agree on the best answer. Ask the team captain to bring the whiteboard to you so you can check for accuracy. Vary the game by giving each team a different sentence with similar kinds of errors for each round.

Sample Topics:

- Punctuation

- Spelling

- Noun-adjective agreement

- Subject-verb agreement in all moods and tenses

- Errors in historical or cultural information written in the target language

Get Around It

Objectives: Use circumlocution to describe a word for another student so he or she can guess what it is.

Materials: List of words for students to describe using circumlocution

Activity Directions and Preparation Hints

This activity works with vocabulary, cultural, and content-based information. Students work in pairs or small groups to guess a word based on another student's description. Each student (or pair if in a small group) is given a list of words he or she must describe for the other student or pair. Students cannot say the word they are describing. This requires the students to use the highly useful skill of circumlocution. These three sentence starters are helpful for having students use circumlocution:

1. It is a place where . . .

2. It is a thing you use to . . .

3. It is a person who . . .

Applications and Modifications

Circumlocution activities can be done at a basic or more complex level. Whatever the level, these activities are useful because students can use this technique to explain something they don't know the word for in the target language. Allow beginning students to write out the description of the word they have to describe before stating it to their partner orally.

Here are a couple of basic examples to get students started using circumlocution at the introductory levels:

- *Book*: The students read it in the library.

- *Teacher*: She teaches the students.

- *Hamburger*: People eat this. It has meat and bread. Sometimes it has cheese, tomatoes, lettuce, and onions.

- *Door*: It opens and closes to enter the house.

- *Kitchen*: It is the place where people cook and eat.

Sample Topics:

- Food

- School supplies

- Rooms in the house

- Verbs

- Passive voice constructions

Happily Ever After?

Objectives: Write the sequel or an alternative ending to a familiar fairy tale.

Materials: Fairy tale in the target language, materials to teach vocabulary in the fairy tale

Activity Directions and Preparation Hints

This activity asks that students write the sequel or an alternative ending to a familiar fairy tale that had a happy ending. Prepare by teaching the students any vocabulary they do not know from the fairy tale you plan to use. Then read the story in the target language. Consider having the students do a cloze activity to review essential vocabulary or grammatical structures from the fairy tale. Use sentences from the story and omit the words you would like students to review. Once students are comfortable with the vocabulary needed, have them write the alternative ending or the fairy tale's sequel. Other extensions include having students act out their fairy tales live or on video with narration. Students could also do an audio recording of their story to practice vocabulary, reading fluency, and pronunciation. An alternative to this is to take a familiar poem from either the student's native language or the target language and modify it or add an additional verse.

Sample Fairy Tales and Poems:

- Cinderella

- Snow White

- Little Red Riding Hood

- Goldilocks and the Three Bears

- The Three Little Pigs

- Jack and Jill

- Little Miss Muffet

- Humpty Dumpty

Hear/Say Activities

Objectives: Listen and find the equivalent of the target language word in English; listen and match an answer to the question you heard.

Materials: Hear/Say activity worksheet

Activity Directions and Preparation Hints

Each student is given a table with two columns (Figure 5.3). Label each table with A or B to distinguish it or use a title of a person, character, or animal to reinforce other vocabulary. The person with the star next to his or her first word begins the activity. At the top of the left column is an ear, and at the top of the right one is a mouth. Students must listen to the word that their partner says, translate it to the other language, find it in their table in the *ear* column, and say the word they see in the *mouth* column right next to it. If the students do the activity correctly, the person that began ends up hearing the word directly next to the starred word where they started the activity. The example in Figure 5.3 includes the activity sheet for both partners and would need to be cut in half along the bold line in the center.

Applications and Modifications

This activity can be used with grammatical topics, vocabulary, cultural, or historical topics. It could even be used with math for multiplication tables and science with the periodic table. This activity was explained using the target and native languages. However, synonyms, opposites, literary characters and their characteristics, words and their definitions in the target language, and various other paired responses could work in the Hear/Say activity. Have students do the activity as you prepare it, or give them a blank grid and ask them to come up with their own activity as a review exercise. After the students finish writing their own, ask them to exchange activities with another pair of students and do the new one.

Sample Topics:

- Questions and answers

- Numbers, alphabet, time, colors, places in the city, or any category of vocabulary

- Countries and capitals

- Professions and the places the people holding the professions work

- Artists and their paintings or styles

- Various forms of conjugated verbs and their meanings in English

- Subject/predicate (find a logical ending to match the subject)

- Review of various facts in a question and answer or fill-in-the-blank type format (Who wrote *Don Quixote*?/The author of *Don Quixote* is . . .)

- Holidays and dates

- Famous people and their contributions

	the librarian 👂👄		the principal 👂👄
	student		pencil
	ruler		teacher
	window		notebook
	eraser		bus
	scissors		books
	pen		calculator
	tape		chair
	folder		crayon

Figure 5.3 Hear/Say Activity Worksheet

Imaginary Room

Objectives: Form questions that elicit a yes or no response.

Materials: Blank sheet of paper

Activity Directions and Preparation Hints

This activity can be used with select grammatical structures, content, and cultural information, as well as any vocabulary that fits in a delineated space. For this activity pair students up and ask them each to make a separate list of 10 items that they would have in their imaginary room. A second option is to allow the students to draw and label the items in the room. You can also do this activity using other spaces, such as a locker, park, suitcase, backpack, basement, car, famous art museum, or concert hall. Direct the students to keep their lists secret from their partners. Once students finish writing their lists, tell them to face one another and begin to ask questions about what is in their rooms. Students should limit their questions to those that can be answered with a yes or no:

- Do you have a bed in your room?

- Are there any shoes?

Begin the activity by telling the students the room they should use or let them pick. If you allow them to choose, the student must figure out what space his or her partner chose. This second option allows for a little more creativity. The students should still ask only yes or no questions:

- Do you eat in the room?

- Is it in a house?

- Is it a kitchen?

- Can you watch a movie there?

- Do you like the place?

Applications and Modifications

Modification 1: Add an Adjective

Materials: Blank sheet of paper

Modify the activity by asking students to write an adjective with each object in the imaginary room. Students guessing the right noun and adjective pair can double their points for the round.

Modification 2: Change the Structure

Materials: Blank sheet of paper

Change the verb or verb tense by having them make a list of things they are going to put, did put, would or would not put, want to put, and so forth in the room and modify the questions being asked accordingly.

Sample Topics:

- Food you would put in the grocery cart if your mom didn't stop you

- Famous Hispanics you would invite to a party if you could

- Things you will take to college for your dorm room

- Habits you won't miss about your sister when she leaves for college

- Works of art (and the name of their artist) you would put in an art museum if you could

- Items you will put in your truck for a camping trip to Michigan with your family

- Things you would put in a suitcase to go to Argentina in July

- Objects a mother thinks her 3-year-old son might have under his bed

Information Gap Activities

Objectives: Ask questions to find out missing information.

Materials: Vary based on the type of information gap activity

Activity Directions and Preparation Hints

An Information Gap activity is any in which some information is missing and the students need to ask questions of other students who have the answers to collect it. This activity can be used with vocabulary, grammatical, cultural, and historical contexts, as well as most academic areas.

Applications and Modifications

Application 1: A/B Activities

Materials: One activity chart for each partner

One example of an A/B activity is one in which students are given a chart with some information missing. Typically, one student is Partner A and the other Partner B. Partners A and B must take turns asking each other questions in the target language to collect the missing information from one another and write it down in their chart. Partner A's chart should include the information that partner B needs and space to write down the information he or she needs. Partner B needs the same chart but with the opposite information as Partner A. Once the information is in the chart, the students have completed the information gap. They can then be asked to extend the practice by writing a summary of their information if applicable, illustrating the information in a picture if they received a description of someone, writing a letter to someone to share what they have learned, and so on. They could also be asked to create an oral presentation to make to the class about the information they have collected.

Sample Topics:

- Question formation and responses

- Past-tense verbs and answers

- Weather

- Personality characteristics

- Hobbies and sports

- Artists and their art styles

- Authors and their works

- Famous musicians and their countries of origin or style of music

- Science or math facts

Application 2: Who/What Am I?

Materials: Set of papers with a different person, place, or thing on it, tape

Students have a paper taped to their back with a person, food, or animal drawn or the name written on it. They must go around the room and ask questions of other students who can see the picture or word to collect information about themselves so they can discover their identity. Students must first greet each other, and then they may start to ask questions about their identity. They cannot ask anyone two questions in a row. Depending on the level and topic, give the students some model questions to ask. The students can come up to you at the end and tell you who/what they think they are for a prize or points. You could also ask them to draw and label a picture of who or what they think they are to turn in to you. They could then compare the picture on their back with the one they drew.

Modification for Who/What Am I?

Materials: Blank sheet of paper

Use this modification with unit-specific vocabulary or as a large-scale review. Put 2–4 words or pictures that are clues to their identities on each student's back. They must ask questions of their classmates so they can figure out all the clues on their back and guess the identity. To save time assign students to draw or write four words that describe a particular person, place, and so forth on a sheet of paper in class right before the activity. Direct students to keep their paper covered so their classmates cannot see it. Give them specific ones to do or allow them to choose their own. When they finish the clues, they should write the answer on the opposite side of the paper. Ask the students to stick the paper on the back of a classmate to avoid having anyone see the clues. Follow the rest of the directions as listed in the original "Who/What am I?" activity description.

Application 3: Self-Portrait

Materials: Picture of a person from clip art, a magazine, or another source, blank sheet of paper, tape

Tape a picture on each student's back. Collect the pictures from magazines, clip art, or drawings. Ask each of your students to bring in a couple pictures to make the collection process easier. Explain to the students that they must collect enough information about the picture on their back to be able to draw a picture of who they are. Once students have collected enough information, they should sit down and draw their self-portrait. When they finish their self-portrait, they can take the original off their back and compare the two. Here are a few extensions for this activity:

- Have students get together in pairs to orally describe their self-portrait to each other.

- Ask the students to present themselves to the class as if they were the person in the original picture.

- Write a brief description of the person they drew, making up hobbies, interests, a profession, and any other information.

Off the Top of My Head . . .

Objectives: Recall vocabulary and write a short story.

Materials: Blank sheet of paper

Activity Directions and Preparation Hints

This activity can be adjusted so students collect information related to vocabulary, grammar, culture, or content by modifying your directions. It requires no advance preparation and is a good review of vocabulary for students. It is also a good indicator of what words the students have retained well. Tell the students to write down the first four words that come into their minds on a sheet of paper. The students must include one noun, one adjective, one verb, and one adverb. Instruct the students to collect 24 (or however many you want) more words from other students. They cannot write down repeat words. Once they have gathered all 24 words, ask them to sit down and do a writing activity that uses them as the main vocabulary source. A few possible topics for using all the words follow:

- 8–10 questions

- A short story

- A letter

- A song

- An ad for a product they have to sell

- Sentences that incorporate as many of the words as they can, with an illustration for each sentence

Applications and Modifications

Application 1: Cultural and Content-Based Uses

Materials: Blank sheet of paper

Ask students to review content-based or cultural information with this activity as well. Direct them to collect the names of elements from the periodic chart of elements and their symbol, a fact about a country, an example of a certain type of verb, a preposition, a food eaten in Nicaragua, a body of water, and so forth. Choose a follow-up activity from the preceding list or design your own.

Or

Objectives: Express and explain opinions.

Materials: List of either/or statements

Activity Directions and Preparation Hints

This activity can be used for vocabulary, grammar, culture, or content review. Prepare a list of 10–30 either/or statements. Adjust the number based on the level you teach and time you have for the activity. They can be as concrete as dog or cat, watch or play baseball, and dance or sing. After you hand out the sheet to students, ask them to begin by circling the one that they agree with on their sheet. Have students either pair up or form small groups and express their opinions in the target language, giving as much of an explanation for the answer as their ability level allows. For lower levels, give the students some key words and phrases to help them to express their opinions and debate a little. Another idea is to project a list from which students can select their preferences.

Applications and Modifications

Application 1: For Advanced Levels

Materials: List of either/or statements

This activity can be good for advanced language students as well. Structure either/or statements to result in more complex discussions. Create questions for upper-level students based on literature students are reading (Who would you rather be, Sancho Panza or Don Quixote?), history (Who was a better leader, Juan or Eva Perón?), and politics (Who makes wiser choices, Democrats or Republicans?). Ask students to write their own either/or statements and then use them with the rest of the class another day. Extend the activity by using it as a springboard for a research project in which the students find more information about an either/or statement. Students can make a presentation, prepare for a debate, or write a paper in the target language.

Sample Topics:

* Animal vocabulary review

* Forms of transportation

* Character traits (Which is more important, being honest or being generous?)

* Review of mixed list of vocabulary from a couple of different units

* Art debate (Who was a more influential art figure, Picasso or Dalí?)

* Favorite holidays (Day of the Dead or Three Kings Day?)

* Grammatical error identification

Order It!

Objectives: Determine the correct sequence of a set of sentences.

Materials: A paragraph in the target language, the original paragraph out of order and cut into sentence strips

Activity Directions and Preparation Hints

This activity lends itself to grammar, vocabulary, content, and cultural topics. Prepare the activity by writing a series of sentences that form part of a paragraph. Write the sentence sequences with a particular vocabulary or grammatical focus. Keep a master sheet with the sentences in order. On the next page of the same document, copy and paste the original sentences in order. Re-arrange them so they are out of order. This sheet with the scrambled sentences is the one to hand out to students. To begin, give each student or pair of students the paper and ask them to cut out the sentence strips. Direct the students to put the sentences in order to form a logical paragraph or story. Circulate through the room so you can verify the order or have a master that students can check once they finish. If you want to extend the activity, ask students to rewrite the paragraph. Make the task more challenging by omitting one of the lines from the paragraph in your sentence strips and ask the students to figure out what sentence is missing. The following are some possible extensions for the activity:

- Change the subject of the sentence and adjust the verb conjugations accordingly

- Change the paragraph from present to past tense

- Add in an adjective for each noun

- Change various details to make the paragraph humorous or illogical

- Translate the paragraph to English

- Add in sentences

- Create a different ending

Applications and Modifications

Application 1: Readings

Materials: A reading, set of sentence strips cut out from the reading

Use this activity to do a cultural or content-based reading in the target language. Once students put the sentences in their correct order, consider having them do one of the following:

- Answer a set of comprehension questions

- Form their own questions about the reading

- Change and add a few sentences in the paragraph to give it a new direction

- Answer oral comprehension questions as a class

Application 2: Songs

Materials: A song, or lines or stanzas of the song cut out in strips

Apply this strategy to song-listening activities. Provide students with strips that correspond to lines of a song. Ask students to listen to the song and correctly order the strips. As an extension, students can try one of the following:

- Translate a stanza

- Change some details to rewrite it

- Rewrite it completely using the same melody

- Write what they think should be the next stanza

- Illustrate the song

- Choreograph dance moves

Application 3: Dialogues

Materials: A dialogue, the dialogue cut up into sentence strips

To model an important dialogue you want students to master, give it to them out of order on the sentence strips. Ask them to put in order, add a couple of new lines of their own, and then memorize the dialogue to present to the class.

Sample Topics:

- Any verb tense

- A song by Celia Cruz

- A section from *Cinderella* in the target language (students can be asked to compare the English and target language version)

- The sequence of events of what happens at Thanksgiving at Grandma's house

- A reading about Mexican muralist Diego Rivera

- Directions for making crepes

- Instructions on how to put together a coffee table

- A dialogue between a store clerk and a customer

Partner Interview and Challenge

Objectives: Form questions; interview a classmate; create a written transcript of an interview; present what was learned about the interviewee to the class.

Materials: List of interview questions

Activity Directions and Preparation Hints

This activity is best applied to vocabulary and grammatical concepts related to students, their interests, and their families. It is a good activity to do either at the end of a unit or at the beginning of a school year to learn about students in your class.

Part 1

In this activity the class brainstorms (or you make a worksheet ahead of time) a list of questions in the target language to ask another student. Although you can do the brainstorm with the entire class, consider having students brainstorm the questions in pairs. Provide the class with a couple of examples to get them started and then ask them to write as many questions as they can with their partner in 5 minutes, after which have the class regroup to make a master list. If you or a student can, type the questions the students propose so you can print or share them electronically. Project the questions so students can see them, follow along, and/or copy them down.

Part 2

On the second day, pass out the list of interview questions to the students. Students must then match up with a classmate they do not know very well to conduct the interview. Both students must communicate entirely in the target language. The interviewer records the answers, and then the students switch roles. For an extension activity, ask the students to do a write-up of the interview and/or present the person to the class orally.

Part 3

Once Part 2 is completed, another option is to have the students find a spot next to each other in the room and sit so they cannot see one another's papers. They should each have a whiteboard and a dry-erase marker or similar tool. Explain to the students that you will be asking them questions about their partner and they should write down a response on their whiteboard. Begin to ask the class questions from the interview list. Both students write as complete of a response as possible in the target language. To determine if the answer is correct, the students show each other their whiteboards and confirm the answers. Remind the students that they must be honest! Students earn a point for each correct response. Students can keep two point tallies: one tally for their points and one for their partner's. At the end of the questioning, the student with the most points wins! Extend by having students write a paragraph about themselves with the answers they gave their partner. They can also take the information they learned about their classmate and put it into paragraph form in the third person. You can also do a combination, where an interviewer writes about his or her classmate, but then the classmate writes a paragraph about him- or herself. That way the two can compare the paragraphs to see if the information is accurate and see the two different verb tenses being employed to write the two different paragraphs.

Sample Topics:

- Family members and pets

- Sports and hobbies vocabulary

- Descriptive adjectives

- The verbs *to be, to live, to have, to do, to make, to like,* and so on

- Question and answer formation

- Present-tense verb conjugation in the first- and second-person singular

- Past-tense verb conjugations in the first- and second-person singular

Roll for It!

Objectives: Practice and recall information about any topic.

Materials: Whiteboards, dry-erase markers, dice

Activity Directions and Preparation Hints

This pair game works well with vocabulary, grammar, culture, and content-related topics. Pair up students for this activity. Each partner needs a whiteboard. When you ask the students a question, they write a response on their whiteboard. The first student of the pair to answer correctly gets to roll the die. Whatever number they roll is the number of points they get for that round. Make the game more interesting by having double bonus rounds, where students who win can double the points they roll or lose triple the points. Make up your own changes at random to keep students interested. Generally, the student with the most points at the end of the game wins; however, some days you can announce that today the student with the least amount of points wins!

Applications and Modifications

Ask students to spell a word; draw a word or scene in the target language; translate a word, phrase or sentence; ask a question for which you give an answer; write a cultural fact; or answer questions about cultural or content-related information.

Sample Topics:

- Professions

- Review of the countries and capitals that speak your target language

- Literary terminology

- Future tense formation

- Vocabulary illustration

Sentence Scramble

Objectives: Create a sentence from a selection of word cards.

Materials: Sheet of paper with various words to be used to form sentences, blank sheet of paper, envelopes, scissors

Activity Directions and Preparation Hints

The Sentence Scramble is a hands-on activity that reinforces sentence formation. Give all students a sheet of paper with the words you want them to use to form sentences. In pairs, ask students to cut out the individual words and then form sentences with the paper slips. As the pairs find sentences, they should write them down on a piece of paper. Create a competition by awarding a small prize to the group with the most logical sentences. Vary it by allowing the sentences to be illogical if they are still grammatically correct. If you intend to reuse the activity, copy the word sets on various colors of cardstock and give students an envelope to put the pieces in when they finish the activity. Ask the students to combine the sentences to make a short paragraph if you have additional time.

Applications and Modifications

Application 1: Including Content and Culture

Materials: Sheet of paper with various cultural or content-based words that form sentences, envelopes, scissors

Although this activity lends itself well to vocabulary and grammatical functions, content and cultural messages can be included in the sentences the students have to put together. See the following examples:

- San José is the capital of Costa Rica.

- Fidel Castro led a revolution in Cuba in 1959.

- One of Velasquez's most famous paintings was *Las Meninas.*

Application 2: Station and Writing Activity

Materials: Typed paragraph in the target language, station markers, small envelopes for each station, each sentence from the paragraph typed up on a separate sheet of paper, envelopes, scissors

Begin by writing or finding a short paragraph that corresponds to the unit's objectives. The paragraph should have as many sentences as the number of stations you want the students to pass through. Keep a master copy of the paragraph and then start a new page in the document for each sentence. Take the words from each sentence and order them randomly on the page, using a larger font so they are easier to use. Print the sentence sheets and place one at each station along with an envelope. Students need more time at the first station so they can cut out the words that will be used by all students at that station. At each station students should take the words out of the envelope, figure out the sentence, write it down, and then put the words back into the envelope. Call rotations until all student pairs or groups have a chance to go to each station. Once the students finish with the station rotations, they should sit down with their partners and try to sequence the sentences into the order of the original paragraph. Pass out the original paragraph that includes a short set of comprehension sentences and have students check their sentences. Students should then reread the paragraph and answer the comprehension questions. Go over the answers with the students or ask them to turn it in as a reading assessment if they answered the questions alone.

Application 3: Verb Conjugation Practice

Materials: Sheet with various subjects and conjugated verbs for each station, blank sheet of paper, envelopes, scissors

Use this activity to have students match subjects and verbs. Give a variety of subjects and many conjugated verbs. Use the same or different verbs. Have the students cut out the verbs and subject pronouns and match them. They should write their combinations on a sheet of paper. This can be done as a station activity or as a seated pair activity.

Sample Topics:

- Sentences that require students to correctly order nouns and adjectives

- Sentences with cultural and/or content embedded in them

- Verbs that require the use of specific pronouns

- Reflexive verbs

- Direct object pronouns used in a sentence

- Sentences that use the past subjunctive; ask pairs to explain why the subjunctive was used in the sentence they formed

Silly Sentences

Objectives: Comprehend sentence meanings; determine if they are logical or not.

Materials: Worksheet with a list of logical and illogical sentences

Activity Directions and Preparation Hints

Use this activity to practice any vocabulary, grammar, culture, or content-related topic. Prepare by writing a worksheet with logical and illogical sentences, using any topic you would like students to review. Pass out the sheet and have the students label the sentences as logical or illogical on the sheet. For more hands-on learners, have the students cut the sentences into strips so they can group them into logical and illogical categories.

Sample Sentences:

- I always wear a banana on my head on Tuesdays.

- My friends fly to school in a jet.

- If I could be anything, I would be an astronaut.

- I brush my teeth while I am sleeping.

- The students walk to school when the weather is nice.

- Dalí was a Spanish president.

Applications and Modifications

Writing Extension

Materials: Blank sheet of paper

Extend the activity by asking students to create their own logical and illogical statements, using their background knowledge or the vocabulary list from the current unit. Ask them to work alone or in pairs. If you have time, allow them to exchange their lists with another group to see if they can figure them out. Have the students share their favorites with the class. Create an additional challenge by asking the students to take your statements or their own new ones and weave them into a short paragraph or story.

Sample Topics:

- Reflexive (verbs)

- Personal hygiene items

- School schedule and ordinal numbers

- A day in the life of _____

- Events of the Spanish Civil War

- Characteristics of and facts about Pablo Picasso

- Personality traits of Don Quixote or Sancho Panza and events of the novel *Don Quixote*

Simple Pair Activities

Objectives: Quiz your partner on a topic to review it.

Materials: Vocabulary list; materials vary for the applications and modifications

Activity Directions and Preparation Hints

After teaching new vocabulary words or grammar to your students, give them a few minutes to quiz each other. This practice serves multiple useful purposes. It allows students to interact with another individual and practice the information in a different way. It also gives the students a chance to identify which words or concepts they still do not know. Oftentimes students ask you questions about what is still unclear as a result of this practice time. This is especially true if you are circulating among them and not sitting at your desk. The basic pair practice gives students additional practice time with the vocabulary and in most cases gives them time to say the words, too. While they practice orally, move through the room to help students pronounce words when you hear them struggling. Try first asking if you can help with the word instead of just offering a correction. It is a friendlier way to give a correction, and I have never had a student say no. Another option is to remember which words are causing most students confusion and to do a quick pronunciation practice of those words at the end of the pair practice time.

Applications and Modifications

This practice is much less complex than the similar activity of the Think/Pair/Share. It can be applied to any topic for which the students have a vocabulary list or notes. The students can practice for a brief period of time or a more extended one.

Application 1: Vocabulary Quizzing

Materials: Vocabulary list

Ask one student to read the vocabulary word in the target language while the other student responds in English. You can also have students provide a sentence or context clue in the target language so students produce the/a desired target language word from it. Have the students switch roles. Then ask students to read or improvise a target language context clue or the English word so the responding student can say the word in the target language. The student listening should be checking the vocabulary list for accuracy and giving polite feedback about the word and/or its pronunciation if possible.

Application 2: Gesture and Vocabulary Practice

Materials: Vocabulary list, gestures for vocabulary words, pictures of vocabulary words posted in the room

If students have learned gestures or have pointed to pictures in the classroom, have them practice these with their partner. One student gives the target language word, and the partner performs the gesture or identifies the picture. Have students switch roles. Make the task more complicated by having one student point to the picture or do the gesture. The responding student then gives the word in the target language.

Application 3: Picture Identification

Materials: Vocabulary list, student drawings of vocabulary words or scenes

Draw or have students draw pictures of the vocabulary that they are learning. Have one student say the word in the target language while the partner points to the correct picture. Challenge students more by having them say the word or phrase that goes with the picture. This approach also works well if you use storytelling as part of your instruction as students can expand and give full sentences to describe a series of pictures or a scene from something you have practiced.

Application 4: Key Question Practice

Materials: List of key questions

Ask pairs to help each other practice or review their key questions. This works best when the students have a list of key questions they can reference. One student begins as the questioner and the partner answers. Have students switch roles. Put a twist on the practice by having the questioning partner provide an answer to the question and the responding student give the correct question.

Modification 1: Pronunciation and Spelling Practice

Materials: Vocabulary list, blank sheet of paper

Have pairs practice pronunciation and spelling by having one student state the word in the target language. The partner's job is to write it down. After they finish they should check the spelling together and switch roles. Partners could also practice by writing down a word in the target language from the vocabulary list and asking their classmate to say the word.

Modification 2: Writing Practice

Materials: Vocabulary list, blank sheet of paper

Change this to a writing activity by having one student say the word in English, do a gesture, or point to a picture while the partner writes down the corresponding word. Switch roles.

Modification 3: Role Plays

Materials: Vocabulary list, list of key questions, role-play cards

Once students have done some basic pair practice of the vocabulary and/or essential grammar, give them role-play cards that reinforce the topic you have been studying. Ask them to write a dialogue or to ad-lib the conversation.

Sample Topics:

- Storytelling vocabulary

- Weather, seasons, colors, days of the week, and so forth

- Verb conjugations (one student gives a subject pronoun and a verb and the partner responds with the conjugation)

- Making plans for the weekend

- Making a phone call

That's Odd!

Objectives: Recognize words that do not fit in a category and explain why they do not.

Materials: Sheet with sets of words where one does not fit in the set

Activity Directions and Preparation Hints

Practice vocabulary, grammar, content, or cultural topics with this activity. It is a good way to review a wide variety of vocabulary and ask students to think about connections between words and language structures. Prepare a sheet with various sets of words in which one does not fit for some reason. When doing the activity, ask students to distinguish the word that does not fit and say or write one or more reasons to explain why it does not. Vary the level of difficulty by combining words that may have very subtle differences or that might have a couple of different ways of combining the words.

Sample Combinations:

- Plant/tree/house/flower (house doesn't fit because it is not alive)

- Dog/cat/horse/bird (bird doesn't fit because it is the only one that flies; it is not a mammal; it has only two legs)

- Blender/refrigerator/whisk/mixer (refrigerator doesn't fit because it doesn't mix things; a whisk doesn't fit because it is not run by electricity)

- Ate/run/skied/skated (run doesn't fit because it is not in the past tense, ate doesn't fit because it is not exercise)

Applications and Modifications

Writing Extension

Materials: Blank sheet of paper

Ask students to write their own word combinations where one word does not fit. Collect them and use some of them as review activities for another day.

Where Is It?

Objectives: Use vocabulary and grammar to guess the location of an object.

Materials: Map or drawing of a specific location, object to hide

Activity Directions and Preparation Hints

This activity is a guessing game. It is particularly good for reviewing vocabulary related to the school, house, city, park, hotel, zoo, restaurant, or any place where there are multiple rooms or locations within one specific space. This activity also reviews prepositions of location and the verb *to be.* You may want to search your favorite image source to find the building or map of locations for the activity. Easily make this a cultural activity by using a map from a target language country subway, zoo, house of a famous person, etc. Students with an iPad or other tablet could also do this activity by pulling up the map on their device from a link you share or by using Google Earth. Another option is for you or a student to draw the building or map of locations before the activity if one of you enjoys drawing.

Once you have the drawing of the location, give students a paper person, animal, or other object for them to hide. Using the house as a sample location, have students guess the room the family dog is in, or to be even more specific have them guess the exact location of the dog in the room. The objective of the game is to be the first to guess where their partner has hidden the person, animal, or object. Play various rounds by simply moving the object to a new location. Extend the activity by having the students try to guess what the person, animal, or object is doing in the particular place they are found. If you would like students to write during the activity, have them record their questions each time they guess and the specific location of the object each time they find it. Writing the sentences helps reinforce the verb *to be* and prepositions of location. Afterward, take a moment to share and discuss the cultural significance of the place you used for the activity.

Applications and Modifications

Application 1: Authentic City Map Navigation

Materials: Authentic map from a city where your target language is spoken, object to hide

Students guess where the object is hidden within the city, using its major landmarks as hiding places. Once it is found, they answer a question from their partner. Do an additional activity with the same map by asking students to orally explain or write directions on how to get from one place to another using the map. Have students research one or more of the places they visited during the activity and write about one or more of them.

Sample Topics:

- Prepositions of location

- Country or other cultural facts

- The verb *to be*

- Vocabulary for the house, city, zoo, school, classroom, park, hotel, museum, restaurant, and so forth

Group Activities

Activity & Brief Description	Page	Application Areas				Type of Communication	
		VO	GR	CO	CU	Oral	Written
Ball Toss Students toss a ball to one another in the classroom as a way to ask questions.	79	•	•	•	•	•	
Chain Stories In small groups, each student writes the first sentence of a story on a piece of paper. Each student then passes the paper to the next person, who adds the next sentence, and so on.	81	•	•	•			•
Chart Swap Students (or the teacher) write a statement or question they would like a response to in a table with other teacher/student questions. The chart gets passed around the room for feedback from other students and then comes back to the owner. Follow up with discussion.	82	•	•	•	•	•	•
Class Sequences Write a sequence of actions for as many students as there are in the class. Students must listen and watch what other students do as their sequence is tied in with those of other students—for example, when you see a person jump, yell, "Goal!"	84	•	•			•	
Firing Line Review material by lining up students in rows so they are face-to-face. Students rotate through and get different questions at each stop.	85	•	•	•	•	•	
Got Your Back Students tape a review sheet to their backs and move around the room contributing and collecting answers from other students for their sheets.	86	•	•	•	•	•	•
Human Sentences Give each student a word on an index card. Students must work together to line up and make a logical sentence.	86	•	•	•	•		

Activity & Brief Description	Page	Application Areas				Type of Communication	
		VO	GR	CO	CU	Oral	Written
Index Card Match Students move around the room asking questions to find matches to their questions or other topics they have on an index card.	88	•	•	•	•	•	
Inside-Outside Circles Form two circles, one inside the other. The inner circle faces out and the outer faces in. Use this format to promote questioning and discussion between students. Students rotate and talk to various classmates.	89	•	•	•	•	•	
Learning Stations Allow students to experience or review information while moving around the room.	90	•	•	•	•		
Lifeboat Ask and answer questions while moving around the room and building relationships.	91	•	•	•	•	•	
Line Up Students are given index cards and asked to line up in order, using only gestures or the target language to find their spots.	92	•	•	•			
Move It! Form a circle with chairs. The student in the center makes a statement. If it applies to students in the circle they must move and find a new seat. The person without a chair stands in the center and makes the next statement.	93	•	•	•	•	•	
Predictions In groups, with questions you provide, students predict how they think each group member would answer the question. Students then discuss the results.	94	•	•	•	•	•	•
Question Chain Sit in a circle with your students. Ask the student next to you a question. That student answers and then repeats the sequence. Use a ball to add interest and mix up the order.	94	•	•	•	•	•	•
Rhythm Use a rhythm to review vocabulary. Students must keep a beat going and say a word that fits the category you are reviewing without missing the beat.	96	•		•	•	•	

Activity & Brief Description	Page	Application Areas				Type of Communication	
		VO	GR	CO	CU	Oral	Written
Snowball Fight! Students write five questions on a sheet of paper. Students ask five different students the questions orally. The students are then allowed to make a snowball from the paper and have a brief snowball fight. Students then pick up a snowball, open it, and write an answer following each question inside. Check the responses for accuracy.	97	•	•	•	•	•	•
Student Investigation Students generate a list of questions they would like answered about their classmates. Each student is given a classmate to investigate and collects answers from other students who know about that person.	98	•	•			•	•
Take a Stand Allow students to show a viewpoint/response to a polarized question by standing on one side of a line or the other.	98	•	•	•	•		
Teacher on the Spot Each student contributes one question they would like you to answer about yourself. Compile the questions. Have all students guess how they think you will respond. Answer their questions the next day.	101	•	•			•	•
Time's Up! Begin the game by asking a question and then tossing an egg timer to a student. The student answers and then tosses the egg timer to another student and asks that student a question. The student who has the timer when it goes off loses a point for his or her team. The team with the least negative points wins.	101	•	•	•	•	•	
Touch Red This group activity is good for practicing colors. Ask students to get out of their seats. Give them a command, such as "Touch red." They have to find something red and touch it. Give another command with a different color.	103	•					

Activity & Brief Description	Page	Application Areas				Type of Communication	
		VO	GR	CO	CU	Oral	Written
Two Truths and a Lie Have students write two true statements and one lie about themselves. Students make guesses about other students. Students practice language and see how well they know their classmates.	104	•	•			•	•
Walk-Around Activities Move around the room, asking questions of other classmates. Write down their responses. Discuss the information collected after the activity.	104	•	•	•	•	•	•
What Is It? The students and teacher sit in a circle with various objects (or their pictures) whose names you want to teach. The student next to you asks, "What is it?" You respond with the name of the object. The student asks, "Is it for me?" You respond, "Yes, it's for you." The sequence continues with the next student. Add additional objects to make it more challenging and fun.	107	•	•	•	•	•	•
Zoo Animals Give each student a slip of paper with the name of an animal on it. Students must close their eyes and move around the room, making the noise of their animal until they find all of the other animals in their group.	108	•				•	

VO = Vocabulary   GR = Grammar   CO = Content   CU = Culture

Ball Toss

Objectives: Ask and answer questions about any topic.

Materials: One soft ball for students to toss to one another

Activity Directions and Preparation Hints

Use this activity to practice any material, including vocabulary, grammar, culture, and content. Students take turns tossing a ball around the room to ask each other questions in the target language. Begin by modeling a particular type of question you want students to answer in the target language. (What do you like to do? What did you do last Friday? What do you want to do this weekend?) The first student asks the question, says the name of a second student, and then throws the ball to that student. The second student catches the ball, answers the question, and asks another question of yet another student. The sequence continues until all students have had a chance or you sense the students are losing interest in the activity.

Applications and Modifications

Application 1: Actions and Words

Materials: One soft ball for students to toss to one another

The first student says a word, and the responding student must do an action that shows the meaning of the word, or vice versa.

Application 2: Translations

Materials: One soft ball for students to toss to one another

The first student says a vocabulary word in English, and the responding student replies with its equivalent in the target language.

Application 3: Where Would You Find It?

Materials: One soft ball for students to toss to one another, paper or whiteboard (optional)

Pass the ball around the room. Upon catching the ball, each student must use the target language to say the name of an object found in a particular room or place that you determine. If using the house as an example, students might say: lamp, cookies, towel, toys, and so on. Students can be eliminated from the round if they cannot provide a response. A couple of students can stand at the board and draw or write the words being said. Involve all students by asking them to write down the words they heard on a piece of paper or whiteboard. Afterward, use the words you collected for writing and drawing activities. Use them to check students' progress with spelling if you had all students write down the words they heard.

Modification 1: Add Another Ball

Materials: Two or more soft balls

Complicate the activity by adding another ball or two to see if students can keep up!

Modification 2: Play in Smaller Groups

Materials: Four or five soft balls

Instead of doing the activity with an entire class, divide students up into smaller groups of six to eight people. Have them stand and form a small circle. They can play using any of the preceding applications. If the students like competition, have them play elimination style. When playing elimination, if students can't respond in 10 seconds, they have to sit down and are out for the round.

Modification 3: Play as a Class Challenge

Materials: One soft ball for students to toss to one another

Use any of the applications for the class challenge. The students can bet you how many correct responses they will have in a predetermined period of time.

Modification 4: Millionaire Version

Materials: One soft ball for students to toss to one another, a play phone

Play a version where you allow students to *phone a friend* if they are unable to answer the question alone. Students can then call on another student to help them answer.

Sample Topics:

- Ask questions that require a yes or no answer.

- Ask information questions that answer question words.

- Name as many Spanish-speaking countries as you can. Try this as a class challenge.

- The first student gives a word and the responding student gives the antonym or synonym.

- Name as many sports as you can.

- Practice present-tense conjugations: The first student asks a question: Do you dance? Do you play an instrument? Do you wear shoes? The responding student must answer, following this type of pattern: Yes, I dance. No, I don't play an instrument. Yes, I wear shoes.

- After doing a cultural study of one of your target language countries, give students a sheet of questions to ask their classmates during a ball toss activity. Name the currency of the country. Who is the president? What is the climate like in May? What is one staple food of the country? What is the capital? Once students finish the oral part of the activity, ask them to individually or in pairs write in answers on the sheet and use it as a study guide. Discuss the answers again with the whole class.

Chain Stories

Objectives: Contribute a sentence to produce multiple group stories.

Materials: Blank sheet of paper

Activity Directions and Preparation Hints

In a chain story each student in a specified pair or group starts by writing a sentence to begin a story. Each student then passes the paper to the next student in line, who reads the previous sentence and then writes another to continue the story. Either predetermine the amount of time allowed for passing the paper or allow the group to progress at its own speed. Continue this way until you call for students to end the activity. Students can then regroup and read all or a sampling of the stories that were written in each group. You may also ask each group to pick their favorite and then stand up and present the story to the rest of the class. Each student in the group should read a couple lines of the story. Ask the class to respond to a few questions after each reading to check for comprehension.

Applications and Modifications

Use the game to practice a current topic being studied, a particular verb tense or structure, or just as a fun review of vocabulary. Use it as a group test review by having the group complete a review sheet together. Have each student complete a section and pass the sheet on. At the end each group should discuss their answers, verify their accuracy, and then share them with the class.

Sample Topics:

- An end-of-the-unit activity to review any topic

- Activities students do in their free time

- A description of a holiday celebration gone awry

- Discussion of what a typical student does/did/would do over the weekend

- The Cinderella story set in the year _____

Chart Swap

Objectives: Propose answers to questions and verify whether they are correct.

Materials: Chart Swap Table (Figure 6.1)

Activity Directions and Preparation Hints

Use this activity to preview, practice, or review any type of vocabulary, grammar, cultural, or content-based information. Any type of question, statement, or word that can fit into a chart works. The chart swap can work as a preassessment, practice, or review activity. Write as many questions, statements, or words as you would like answers for in the first column of the Chart Swap Table. Students should begin by writing their name on their paper. Students are to answer one of the questions in the *Proposed Answer* column and pass the table to another student. In the second round, the student first looks at the answer the previous student wrote for the preceding question and decides if he or she agrees with the answer. In the column marked *Do you agree?* the student writes yes or no. Next, the student answers a new question in the table and passes the table to another student. The third student to receive the chart looks at the previous two answers, marks a response in the *Do You Agree?* column for both questions, and answers a new question. This continues until all questions have been answered and assessed to see if other students agree. Students need to assess only three of the previously answered questions. They do not need to mark an opinion for every answer on the sheet. Allow students to share their answers in pairs or small groups briefly. If they need to, they should come to a consensus on their answers. Come back together as a class for a whole-group discussion of the answers, and provide time to clarify any questions that arose during the activity. During this time the students should listen and fill in the correct answer to the question in the *Correct Answer* column. If the sheet was filled in as a way to review for a test, students can take it home and review the information.

Applications and Modifications

This is a nice way to review topics from class because it gives students a chance to move around and think about their own answers, as well as those of other students. One way to use this same activity and involve the students more is by having them generate the questions. Provide the students with a blank table and have the same table projected for the class to see. Take questions from students and write them down for the rest of the class to copy down in their blank table.

Questions	Proposed Answers	Do You Agree?			Correct Answers
1.					
2.					
3.					
4.					
5.					
6.					
7.					
8.					
9.					
10.					
11.					
12.					

Figure 6.1 Chart Swap Table

© *Activities, Games, and Assessment Strategies for the World Language Classroom*, Amy Buttner Zimmer, Taylor & Francis

Sample Topics:

- Write down an answer to a key oral question on which students will be given an oral test.

- For a test on the Mexican celebration of Day of the Dead, write questions about parts of the celebration you want students to review and discuss.

- Write the name of the holiday that goes with the date provided.

- Write the name of an object and have the receiving students provide descriptions of or uses for it.

- Have students write a brief description of a literary figure or answer a question about their reading.

Class Sequences

Objectives: Students watch and listen for cues in the target language and react to them.

Materials: Class sequence slips

Activity Directions and Preparation Hints

Use the game to practice different command forms and topical vocabulary, and as a review of previously studied vocabulary. In this group activity, each student is given a slip of paper with a direction, such as "Write your name on the whiteboard." One student begins by doing what the slip directs them to do. Other students watch what the student does and check their slips. For this example the student whose slip reads, "After someone writes their name on the whiteboard, get up and dance" does their action next. Other students watch for the next cue and are ready. The student whose paper has the statement, "After you see someone dance, stand up, yell 'Oh no,' and sit back down" follows the direction. Make sure to have enough slips for everyone, and when the last person goes, the chain ends. Keep a master sheet handy in case any confusion arises during the activity. If you would like to use them with other classes, be sure to collect all of the slips.

Applications and Modifications

Writing Extension

Materials: Blank sheet of paper

Individually, in pairs, or in groups, students can write their own sequence of commands for the class to do in subsequent class periods. For an easier variation, ask students to write commands for the whole class to perform simultaneously. Students can also write sequences for classes that are more novice than they are to review previously taught material and to provide a real audience for their work.

Sample Topics:

- Formal and informal command sequences

- Action verbs

- Classroom vocabulary

Firing Line

Objectives: Respond to questions to review any topic.

Materials: Set of questions and correct responses on index cards

Activity Directions and Preparation Hints

This activity lends itself well to being used with vocabulary, grammar, content, or cultural applications. The Firing Line requires a bit of room reorganization, but it has multiple applications. Set up for the activity by lining up chairs or desks so that the students will be face-to-face. Make sure that there is a seat for each student. One way to structure this activity is to divide the students into an X and a Y side. Give the X students a question, a situation card, a role, or other task on paper. Student X directs the questioning or review. Give each X student two or three questions that the Y student has to answer. Give the X student the question and answer so they can give the Y student feedback if needed. Call a rotation and have the students move one seat to the left. Students repeat the cycle with another X student, who has different questions. To avoid having the X students ask the same questions over and over, have the X student pass the question card to the right as students rotate to the left, thus avoiding repeat questions. Once the X students get their original question back, they become Y students and switch roles. If you would like to have students take more ownership in the writing of the questions, ask them to write them a day or two before so you can pick the best ones and/or verify their accuracy. If students are more adept at writing the questions, you may consider having pairs of students write the questions and answers immediately prior to the activity. Quickly check their work for accuracy and begin the activity. This activity could work nicely as a review game at the beginning of the year to refresh some prior material or to review at various points during the year.

Applications and Modifications

If the class is larger and the tasks at each station are longer, as is the case with role-plays, consider giving out only three to five different situation cards or dialogues. This allows for smaller sets of separate desk or chair rows or more than one chance to practice.

Sample Topics:

- Review for a test or final exam.

- Do a practice session of key oral questions before a test or final exam.

- Do a review of multiple role-play or other short dialogue situations.

- Complete an interview of a student using multiple interviewees.

- Debate the same or different topics with various students.

- Conduct a job interview.

- Discuss questions about a book.

- After writing a composition for class, do a read-around. Every pair of students has a copy of their own work. The pairs switch and provide feedback to one another informally or on a form you provide.

Got Your Back

Objectives: Respond to questions about any topic.

Materials: Review worksheet, tape

Activity Directions and Preparation Hints

Use this activity to reinforce vocabulary, grammar, culture, or content-based information the students have learned. Give students an interactive review of unit information by creating a one-page review sheet of key information. Have students tape the sheet to their back. They need to walk around the room, sharing the information for the answers they know by writing one answer down on the sheet on each student's back. In the meantime they collect information from other students on the sheet on their own back. Once students finish, they should remove the review sheet from their back and sit down. Have students share the answers they have, correct any errors, and discuss any questions about the information that arise. Vary the review sheet by asking students to provide a vocabulary word, sentence translation, answer to a question, or the question for the answer written on the sheet.

Sample Topics:

- Label the parts of a house and items in it.

- Identify pictures of vocabulary words.

- Answer questions about activities that are popular in winter.

- Identify sample works of art with the name of the painting or artist.

- List objects you would find in certain places (in a second grader's backpack, in a middle school boy's locker, in the family medicine cabinet, in the kitchen sink, in the refrigerator after Christmas dinner, in the garage, in a suitcase for a trip to Iceland, etc.). List various places on the sheet or stick to one and have each student add a couple of items.

- Conjugate verbs in any tense.

Human Sentences

Objectives: Form sentences with words written on 3×5 cards.

Materials: Sets of index cards, each card with one word on it, that when combined with other cards from the set form a sentence

Activity Directions and Preparation Hints

The Human Sentences activity reinforces sentence structure. To begin, write a series of sentences that fit into what you are teaching or reviewing. Then take the sentences and write each word from the sentence on an index card. Clip the cards together or put them into an envelope to keep the sentences separated. Alternatively, you can write on colored index cards or cardstock that is cut to the size you want to color-code. Printing out the words from your sentences is also another option. It is helpful to write each set of cards in a different color so you can easily return a misplaced card to its original set. For an additional challenge, add a word into the sentence that doesn't belong and have students determine which one it is.

If you don't have time to prepare the sentences, ask students to write various sentences with the verbs and vocabulary you would like them to include. Check their work and then have them transfer the words to the index cards. This works well as a station activity. Students can rotate from set to set. Ask students to write down the sentences that their group formed on a sheet they number or letter based on how you label the stations.

Applications and Modifications

This activity is primarily useful for practicing vocabulary and grammar. Cultural and content-based information can be included in the sentences as well. The strength of this activity is that it gets students out of their seats and thinking about the correct order of sentences and the meanings of the words to create a logical sequence. Extend this activity by having students write a story or letter into which they have to incorporate a specific number of the sentences they formed during the activity.

Modification 1: Instead of doing this as a station activity, create two teams. Give each team a set of cards. If you give each team the numbers 0–9, you can call out number or math problems for groups to solve. The first team to run to the front and have their numbers in the correct order wins the round. It is helpful to write down the numbers or math problems you plan to use ahead of time. Students can also just write out the numbers or problems you call out on a whiteboard as an alternative if the running gets out of hand.

Modification 2: Give teams a set of letters. Make sure to offer duplicates of high-frequency letters used in your language or limit yourself to words that do not require multiples of the same letters in a word. Try focusing on words that students tend to misspell or on other unit-related (current or prior or a mix of both) terms. Students need to form the word and run to the front to try to form their word before the other team does. You can call out the words in English, or you can create more of a challenge by describing the word with circumlocution, creating a cloze situation the word would fit in or asking a question that would result in that answer. Opt to show the word, situation, or question on the board for visual support as well, or just provide an oral prompt. The website www.quizlet.com can be very handy for showing a visual prompt for your questions. If you prefer not to use the letters or they are not readily available, have one or a pair of students from each team run to the board and spell the word with a marker on their side of the board.

Sample Topics:

- Telling time

- Math problems

- Working with difficult-to-spell words

- Noun-adjective agreement

- The conditional tense

- Direct and indirect object placement

- Reflexive verb formation

Index Card Match

Objectives: Find the correct answer to a question by interacting with other students.

Materials: Class set of question and answer cards

Activity Directions and Preparation Hints

Begin by making a set of questions and answers. Write a question on one index card and its answer on a separate one. Continue making cards until you have enough question and answer cards for each student in the class. Pass out either a question or an answer card to each student. A quick way to do this might be by putting your questions and answers into Quizlet and then using the Print feature to print out index card–size flashcards that have your content on them.

To begin, direct the students to interact with one another to find the answer to the question they were given on their index card. The students with a question must walk around the room and ask the question, and the students with an answer card must respond with the answer on their card. The two students need to determine if their cards are a logical match. If they are not, the students keep looking. Once two students find that they are a pair, they sit down together. At this point they can be asked to wait until the other students finish, or they can be given a task to complete together. One option could be to ask pairs to come up with the questions and/or answers for the activity they were just working on. You could provide a question or answer and ask for the missing information. You could also provide a prompt in English for them to determine the missing question and/or answer. At some point after all students have finished, you can have the pairs take turns asking their questions of the class and getting one of the students in the audience to answer. This can work as a nice review of oral questions for your unit. Once the activity is done, collect the index cards for future use. Once again, www.quizlet.com may be helpful for printing out the questions if you would like to have them available online for future use.

Applications and Modifications

Use this activity with any vocabulary, grammar, culture, or content. Modify the activity from the original version by having students match artists and their works, authors and their books, famous Hispanics and their contributions, subjects and predicates, items and their uses, and so forth. This activity also serves as a nice way to pair up students for any subsequent activity. Provide the students with a written activity to reinforce the first oral one or move on to something different.

Sample Topics:

- Questions and answers

- Pairs of opposites

- Pairs of synonyms

- Objects and a description of their uses

- Items and what you need to make them

- Composers and their pieces

- Foods and the country with which they are most associated

- Presidents and their countries

- A musical genre and its country of origin

Inside-Outside Circles

Objectives: Respond to questions on any topic.

Materials: Varies, depending on how you use the activity

Activity Directions and Preparation Hints

In this activity students interact with many different students. Have students form two circles, one inside the other. The students in the outside circle face in and those in the inner circle face out, so they are face-to-face with another student. Provide the students with directions as to what type of exchange you intend for them. Call a rotation and have the students on the inside move one space clockwise so they have a new partner.

Applications and Modifications

Students can converse about any topic, from vocabulary to content-related material. Some possible applications of this activity include having students quiz each other on vocabulary words using flashcards or their vocabulary list, do gestures they have learned that correlate to vocabulary words or phrases, practice key questions, perform short dialogues, and quiz each other on essential information or grammatical topics. Guide the review by giving the students flashcards, situation cards, or other cue cards to make sure they know what to do. For a quick vocabulary review, use your classroom set of flashcards and give one or more to each student in the inner circle so they can quiz the student in the outer circle. If you use Quizlet, you can easily print out the vocabulary flashcards from its Print menu. Designate whether they should give their answer in English or the target language. Depending on the number of students in your class, you may want to have students form more than one circle.

Making the Cue Cards

Materials: Index cards, cardstock, or regular paper

Use the cue card to write a word or question, guide a dialogue, or give the students a situation. The cue card should have the question on one side and the answer on the other. Consider making the cue cards on index cards or cardstock so you can use them multiple times. A second option for the cards is to type and print the questions and answers on regular paper. If you are short on preparation time and want to challenge your students more, give them enough guidance so they can write the cue card.

Application 1: Keep the Cue Card

Materials: Cue cards

Begin by giving each student in the inner circle a cue card. The student keeps the card and asks the question, has the dialogue, or practices the situation on the card with each student who rotates through. Once students rotate through the entire circle, the student with the card passes that card to his or her current partner in the outer circle and they switch spots. Now the student who was previously in the inner circle is part of the outer and goes through the rotation, receiving the questions and answering them.

Application 2: Pass the Cue Card

Materials: Cue cards

An alternative to Application 1 is to have the student in the inner circle pass the cue card counterclockwise as the student in the outer circle moves clockwise. Once the student in the outer circle arrives back to the original question, the activity stops.

Sample Topics:

- Review vocabulary from a unit on the family.

- Have students greet one another and ask each other how they are doing.

- Have students ask each other what they did over the weekend.

- Provide students with a staple food and ask them to identify a country where it is eaten.

- Show students a date and ask them what holiday it is.

- Show students a word and ask them to use circumlocution to describe it.

- Give the name of a literary character and have students identify the book they are from, their main traits, their fatal flaws, and so forth.

- Give the student the name of an important historical figure and have them identify his or her role or contribution.

- Students quiz each other on countries and capitals, or flags and countries of the target language culture.

- Students have a brief dialogue about what they will do after school today.

Learning Stations

Objectives: Recall and practice vocabulary while moving around the room.

Materials: Stations set up in the room with different tasks to do at each one, review sheets or notebook paper

Activity Directions and Preparation Hints

To prepare for this activity, label and set up stations around the classroom where students complete different tasks. Create a review sheet ahead of time where students can record their answers from each station or simply have them write them on notebook paper. Leave time at the end to discuss the answers.

Applications and Modifications

Practice vocabulary, grammar, culture, history, or any other content with this activity. It is more interactive because it allows the students to get up out of their seats. Set a time limit per station, and call rotations or let students work at their own pace.

Sample Station Topics:

- Answer the five questions at Station A on your review sheet. Use the pictures at the station to guide the answers.

- Write five questions about the pictures at Station B.

- Identify the 10 pictures at Station C.

- Identify the artists of the five paintings at Station D.

- Write a dialogue with six lines to introduce one friend to another at Station E.

- Look at the clocks at Station F and write down the times.

- Identify the famous explorers at Station G.

- Measure the cultural items in the unit of measure of the target country at Station H and record your findings.

Lifeboat

Objectives: Respond to questions about any topic.

Materials: Set of questions to project, enough 11×14 sheets of construction paper for half of your class, *Jaws* or other appropriate theme song

Activity Directions and Preparation Hints

Use this activity to get students to interact and speak to one another in the target language. Before beginning, create a set of questions to project and have enough pieces of 11 × 14 construction paper for two students to fit on each one. Google Presentation works nicely for preparing your questions as you can later share the presentation with students if you would like them to respond to the questions as written homework. Begin the activity by playing the theme song from the movie *Jaws.* Students *swim* around the room until the music stops, at which point they must hurry to a lifeboat (indicated by a piece of construction paper). Once students are on the lifeboat, direct them to answer a question or discuss a topic you have. When the music starts again, all students start swimming. As the activity progresses, continue to remove lifeboats. As there are fewer boats, more students must squeeze onto one, holding onto one another to make sure the shark doesn't eat anyone.

Applications and Modifications

Use the lifeboat activity to practice any material. Tailor the questions to the level of the student and the topic being studied or reviewed. Modify the name of the activity so you can ask students to do a different action or make it fit your topic. You might call it *In the Trees*, and then students would have to be birds flying or monkeys swinging from tree to tree.

Sample Topics:

- What do you like to do?

- Who is your favorite musician?

- If you were president, what would you change?

- What did you do last weekend?

- Who was your favorite character in *Don Quixote* and why?

- Name a Spanish-speaking country and its capital.

- Name an indigenous civilization in Mexico and one characteristic of it.

- Give a synonym or antonym for the word *small*.

- State three forms of transportation.

Line Up

Objectives: Put sequential items in order.

Materials: Set of index cards with sequential items

Activity Directions and Preparation Hints

Use this activity to introduce, practice, or review items that occur in a sequential order. Give students index cards with the months, days of the week, dates, numbers, and so forth, and ask them to line up in order. Make the activity more complicated by telling students they may not talk to each other at all or they may use only actions and the target language to communicate.

Applications and Modifications

Although this is a good activity to get students up and moving and as a way to introduce a new topic, it is limited to things that occur in a particular sequence. Extend the activity beyond sequential vocabulary by asking students to put historical events in order. Also use it to have students order directions for making or doing things. Try it with a short story or book by having students put the main events in chronological or even reverse order.

Sample Topics:

- Days of the week

- Numbers

- Dates

- Months

- Sequence to follow for baking a cake

- Description of one's daily routine

- Directions for washing dishes

- Timeline of historical events

- Order in which presidents served

Move It!

Objectives: Make and react to statements in the target language.

Materials: Enough chairs for each of your students

Activity Directions and Preparation Hints

Begin by arranging a circle or circles of chairs so you have enough for all students. Ask the students to find a chair and sit down. Model the activity by standing in the center of the circle. Make the equivalent statement in the target language:

- My name is . . .

- Move if you . . . (like ice cream, love soccer, want to go to Mexico, etc.)

If the statement is true about a student, he or she gets up and finds a new seat. Everyone who has to move to a new seat needs to find one that is at least three places away from their previous spot. The person standing in the middle also needs to find a seat. Whoever is left out is the new person in the middle and makes the next statement. Encourage students to practice their listening skills by asking them to listen for either things they did not know about other students or things they have in common with people that they did not realize. This is a good activity to do if you have restless students who need to get up and out of their seats for a few minutes because it does not require advance preparation.

Applications and Modifications

This activity can be used to practice particular language functions, such as likes, preferences, things students want to do in the future, and so forth.

Application 1: Reviewing Content

Materials: Enough chairs for each of your students

Ask the student in the middle to make a true or false statement. Direct students to move if they agree with the statement. For example, George Washington was the eighth president; move if you think Paris is the capital of France. Briefly pause in between rounds to clear up any confusion about the statements. Play the activity until you sense that students are losing interest or you are out of time.

Sample Topics:

- Items in the house, places in the city, items you need for a trip, and so on when included in a statement (e.g., "Once I broke the toaster"; "I never go to the library"; "I always take a frog when I go on a trip")

- Formation of statements with "I like" and "I don't like"

- Statements with reflexive verbs about one's daily routine ("I always brush my teeth"; "I never wash my toes"); encourage students to mix in illogical or silly statements for creativity and to see if other students are really comprehending the statements.

- True and false statements for topics related to content or culture

- Favorite books or literary characters

- Artists and their artwork or songs

- Famous architects and their buildings

Predictions

Objectives: Make predictions about expected responses to certain questions from a classmate. Confirm or disprove the predictions by asking the student the question and comparing the response with the predicted one.

Materials: Set of questions for students to answer, predictions table for recording answers (Figure 6.2)

Activity Directions and Preparation Hints

Form groups of three to four students who don't know each other well. Begin by giving students the predictions table (Figure 6.2), adapted to your language and topic. Direct them to predict how each person in the group will answer the questions listed in the left column. After students make their predictions, the group should take turns asking the questions of each other and see how many of their predictions were correct. As classmates respond, each group member should record his or her answers in the corresponding location of the chart.

Applications and Modifications

Use this activity to practice any type of oral question in the target language. Differentiate for more advanced students, or give the whole class more of a challenge by asking each of them to write six to eight of their own questions. Students can write the questions as individuals, and then the group can decide on the ones they want to use, or the group can simply work together to write them. Once they finish, they should inform you so you can check their work for accuracy before they begin making their predictions. Direct the students to write a specific type of question or let them choose. Depending on the level of your students, you may want to make more basic questions off-limits. If working collaboratively in small groups, Google Docs can be helpful so all students can contribute. If students share the document with you, you can have tabs open for all of the groups and be following their progress and commenting via your computer.

Question Chain

Objectives: Ask and answer questions about any topic.

Materials: A question or questions you would like students to practice

Activity Directions and Preparation Hints

The objective of this activity is to practice asking and answering questions. For this to work effectively, spend some time modeling the questions you want the students to ask before doing this activity. Direct a student to begin the activity by asking the student seated to his or her right a question. The second student gives a response and asks the same question of the student to his or her right.

Question	Student 1	Student 2	Student 3
What is your favorite color?	Prediction:	Prediction:	Prediction:
	Correct answer:	Correct answer:	Correct answer:
How old are you?	Prediction:	Prediction:	Prediction:
	Correct answer:	Correct answer:	Correct answer:
What is your favorite activity?	Prediction:	Prediction:	Prediction:
	Correct answer:	Correct answer:	Correct answer:
How many cats do you have?	Prediction:	Prediction:	Prediction:
	Correct answer:	Correct answer:	Correct answer:
What is your middle name?	Prediction:	Prediction:	Prediction:
	Correct answer:	Correct answer:	Correct answer:
What is your favorite season?	Prediction:	Prediction:	Prediction:
	Correct answer:	Correct answer:	Correct answer:
What was your favorite vacation?	Prediction:	Prediction:	Prediction:
	Correct answer:	Correct answer:	Correct answer:
How many places have you lived?	Prediction:	Prediction:	Prediction:
	Correct answer:	Correct answer:	Correct answer:
What is your least favorite food?	Prediction:	Prediction:	Prediction:
	Correct answer:	Correct answer:	Correct answer:
What is your favorite book?	Prediction:	Prediction:	Prediction:
	Correct answer:	Correct answer:	Correct answer:

Figure 6.2 Predictions

Applications and Modifications

Use the activity to practice vocabulary and grammar through question formation. Vary the activity by having more than one question passing through the circle at a time. Use a ball to vary the order of students responding to the questions. Be careful not to structure questions that require a complicated response if you want the question to pass through the circle quickly. If this is too basic for your level of students, ask students to have their own question ready for the next person. Vary the level of difficulty of the questioning based on your group of students. Add written practice by asking the students to write down the question(s) they were asked and their answers. Check their work for accuracy.

Sample Topics:

- What is your name?

- How are you?

- What will you do tomorrow?

- What did you do last weekend?

- Where did you go yesterday?

- What do you like to do in the summer?

- What did you see when you were on vacation?

Rhythm

Objectives: Review a topic to a rhythmic beat.

Materials: None; however, you may want to use flashcards to review the vocabulary you want to practice before this activity.

Activity Directions and Preparation Hints

Pick a category of vocabulary or verbs you would like to review. For the example, use family members as a category. Begin by demonstrating the following beat. On beat 1 pat your thighs once, on beat 2 clap your hands, on beat 3 snap your fingers on your left hand once, and on beat 4, snap your fingers on your right hand. On beats 3 and 4 say something that fits in that category like (my brother), one word per snap. To begin, a student calls out a category. The next student must add a word that fits in the category without missing a beat. Start over if the beat is lost. Students may call category changes throughout the game. Play the game with students sitting in a circle or at their desks. Designate a pattern of going up and down rows or have students point to the next person.

Applications and Modifications

Play this after students have had enough practice with the vocabulary to think and respond quickly. A brief review of flashcards or a vocabulary brainstorm on the board helps reactivate the students' memory and makes the game more successful. A secondary way to play the game is to have students state all the words preceding theirs before they add their new word. Also play by having the whole group repeat the statement made by the student whose turn it is on the last two beats. For example, if the student says, "my brother," the class snaps for each word and says, "my brother" on the two beats that follow immediately afterward. The game continues with the next person.

Sample Topics:

- Reflexive verbs

- Regular present tense verbs or their endings

- Personal hygiene objects

- Animals

- Favorite foods

- Things to do on a Saturday afternoon

- Things you wouldn't want to take on vacation

Snowball Fight!

Objectives: Ask and answer questions on any topic.

Materials: Blank sheet of white paper for each student

Activity Directions and Preparation Hints

The snowball fight is a way to practice questions and answers, as well as any other topic. Choose a certain number of questions, and ask students to write them on a piece of paper. Give them a specific type of question you would like them to practice or leave their options open. Go around the room, check the questions for accuracy, and provide the students with feedback. To speed up your checking, have them first show the questions to their partners to see if they find any errors. For more novice students, provide questions for them to choose from on the board that they can copy from you. You can also provide them with a few different versions of sheets with questions that are already prepared. Once the questions have been checked, direct the students to orally ask their questions of other students in the classroom. Once they have done this, the students may wad up their paper into a *snowball*. Allow students about a minute to throw *snowballs* at each other. Tell them they cannot throw the *snowballs* at anyone's head. Once the time is up, direct students to pick up a *snowball*, open it, and write down a complete answer for all of the questions on the paper. Check the students' work and provide feedback. A second possibility is to have students ask their classmates the questions they wrote and record their responses.

Applications and Modifications

This activity works well with vocabulary, grammar, culture, and content information. Students especially enjoy the activity because they get to have a *snowball fight.* It is a good way to get them up and moving and provides a way to do a quick check for comprehension of any topic you want to practice.

Sample Topics:

- Form and answer *who* questions.

- Form and answer second-person singular questions in the past tense.

- Write questions about a section of a story or book that students just read.

- Write down the five most challenging questions from the unit.

- Write true and false statements about a country that students just studied.

Student Investigation

Objectives: Ask and answer questions about other students in the classroom.

Materials: Student Investigation Chart (Figure 6.3)

Activity Directions and Preparation Hints

Instead of conducting a traditional one-on-one interview, make or have students create a set of questions to help them learn about another student in the class. Brainstorm the questions together and write them into the table. After the questions in the table are complete, the student is in charge of collecting that information about his or her partner from other students in the class without ever talking to the partner. If a student does not know the answer, the interviewer must find another student who can answer the question. At the end of the activity, the interviewer should ask his or her partner any questions he or she could not answer and verify that the collected answers are in fact correct. Ask the students to prepare a written description of their partner to present to the class or do an impromptu presentation, just using their notes from the activity. As a challenge ask the class if anyone is able to present you to the class, using the same questions from the chart.

Applications and Modifications

Depending on the level of your students, vary the type of questions the students ask about one another. A specific or variety of grammatical structures can also be practiced with this activity.

Sample Topics:

- Questions about the student's family, pets, interests, likes/dislikes, favorites

- Questions about the student's future plans (could be for the weekend, summer, college, etc.)

- Questions about what the student did over a holiday break (this could involve the interviewees conjecturing about what they think the student did)

- Questions about if the student could go anywhere, be any person, have any profession, where/who/what would it be

Take a Stand

Objectives: Respond to statements about any topic by moving to one side of the room or the other.

Materials: Set of questions, masking tape

Questions	Answers	Name of Student Who Answered
1.		
2.		
3.		
4.		
5.		
6.		
7.		
8.		
9.		
10.		
11.		
12.		

Figure 6.3 Student Investigation Chart

Activity Directions and Preparation Hints

Prepare a list of statements that review any topic the students are studying or have studied. Tape a line of masking tape on the floor to make two sides of the room or draw an imaginary line to divide the class. To begin, direct students to stand on either side of the line. Indicate which side of the line means students agree with the statement and which is for disagreement. Write a plus sign on one side of the board to indicate that people who stand on that side of the line agree and a minus sign on the other side of the line to indicate disagreement with the statement. Start the activity with one of the statements you wrote. Students decide their response and move to the appropriate side of the line. Statements can be as simple as I have a brother, I have a pet, I wash the dishes at my house, and so forth. More complex ideas can be explored as well. This is a quick way to ascertain students' viewpoints on important issues without them ever having to say anything. Use this activity to practice listening comprehension and to allow students to move around. Continue until you finish or students lose interest.

Applications and Modifications

This is another flexible activity that can be applied to vocabulary, grammar, culture, or content review. Also use it as a way to quickly divide students up to have a quick pair activity. Students talk with people who have similar ideas if they talk to someone standing on their side of the line or discuss with someone their conflicting views by picking someone on the opposite side of the line.

Application 1: Divide Students into Groups

Materials: Set of questions

Use this activity as a way to divide students into groups for any activity. Ask as many questions as you would like before creating the groups. Remind students that they move based on their opinion or what they think the answer is. Encourage them not to move based on what their friends or other students are deciding.

Modification 1: Students Ask Questions

Materials: Set of questions

Give students the chance to practice speaking skills with this activity as well. Direct students to ask someone on their side of the line a question in the target language each time they move. Ask them to ad-lib questions or assist them by posting questions on the board as soon as they move sides. Practice the same question more than once or a different one each time.

Sample Topics:

- Vocabulary and grammatical functions of expressing things students love, like, and dislike—e.g., I like to swim; I really dislike eating fish.

- True and false statements work as a pre- or postassessment.

- Practice any type of questioning and answering in the target language. As a follow-up, once students pick a side of the line, have them ask each other a question before you ask your next one.

- Discover students' values.

- Express opinions about controversial topics.

Teacher on the Spot

Objectives: Form questions to which the teacher will respond; allow students to learn about the teacher.

Materials: Table for recording questions and answers (Figure 6.4)

Activity Directions and Preparation Hints

Begin by having the students write down three questions they would like you to answer about yourself, in the target language if possible. Let the students know that they should be questions they would be willing to answer about themselves and appropriate for school. Ask students to form groups of five, share their questions, and make sure that they do not have any repeat questions among them. Ask a spokesperson from each group to raise a hand and ask you the questions. Write the questions down on the board for the students to see. If you have a projector, type the questions into your computer and project the questions on a screen. As you write the questions, ask the students to copy them down onto their own sheet of paper, leaving a space for the answer, or use Figure 6.4. After all of the questions have been posed, ask the students to write down what they think your answer will be. Afterward, ask the students to take turns asking the questions on the list. As you answer, the students should record your response. Write down your answer so students can see it for correct spelling. Ask the students to give themselves one point for each answer they got correct. The student with the most correct answers wins a prize.

Applications and Modifications

This activity is best used with a vocabulary and/or grammatical application in mind. Although its primary purpose is to give the students a chance to get to know you a little better, it can be used as a model for students to then share about themselves. As an extension, take the questions the class submitted, type them up, and make copies. Ask the students to answer the questions about themselves so you can also learn about your students. Use this activity at various points in the year as students learn more questions. Using the activity more than once will also give you and your students a chance to learn more about each other.

Sample Topics:

- Practice questions that require a yes or no response.

- Practice question words.

- Review personal characteristics, family members, likes/dislikes, hobbies, and sports.

- Use as a way to review questions from multiple units.

- Modify the activity for use with the past tense to ask about what you were like or did as a child/middle school student/high school student.

- Have the students answer the questions they asked you about themselves and write up a paragraph or do a brief oral presentation. Ask their classmates to fill in a grid with a bit of information on each presenter as they listen.

Time's Up!

Objectives: Ask and answer questions about any topic.

Materials: Egg timer

Question	Predicted Answer	Actual Answer	Points
1. Where are you from?			
2. What is your favorite sport?			
3. What do you like to do?			
4. How old are you?			
5. Do you have siblings?			
6. How old are your siblings?			
7. What are their names?			
8. What is your favorite color?			
9. What is your favorite food?			
10. Where do you like to eat?			
11. Do you like onions?			
12. Do you have a pet? What kind?			
13. Do you like to read?			
14. What is your favorite book?			
15. What is your favorite movie?			
16. Who is your favorite actor?			
17. What do you do on the weekend?			
Total Points:			

Figure 6.4 Teacher on the Spot

Activity Directions and Preparation Hints

This activity promotes oral communication in a large group setting. You will need an egg or other timer that is easy to toss. Have students form a circle and split the circle into two teams. Set the timer for an amount of time you determine. Begin the activity by asking a question and then tossing the egg timer to another student. That student must answer the question, ask a new one, and then pass the timer on to another student. The questioning and answering continue until the egg timer goes off. Whoever has the timer in hand when it goes off loses a point for the team. The team with the least amount of negative points at the end of the game wins. This keeps students on their toes and the questions and answers flowing because they won't want to be caught with the timer. You may want to make the rule that the timer cannot be passed to the same person more than once in one round.

Applications and Modifications

Use this activity with vocabulary, grammar, culture, or content-based questioning. Determine ahead of time the types of questions students should ask, and model a few on the board if it is a question or structure with which they are unfamiliar. Have students practice asking and answering the question(s) with other classmates before beginning. Listen as they practice so you can help them with any pronunciation errors. If you want the activity to be more challenging and a good review of previously taught material, tell students that they can use any question they have learned.

Modification: Teacher-Provided Question List

Materials: List of questions

Before the activity, provide students with a list of questions that they have learned to reactivate their memory. Allow the students to look over the list and practice with their classmates. Also allow time for them to ask you any clarification questions about meaning or pronunciation. Once the competition begins, do not allow the students to use their sheets, unless you have beginner language students who are not yet comfortable forming their own questions under pressure.

Sample Topics:

- What's your favorite . . . ?

- What do you like to do?

- What did you eat for breakfast today?

- Where do you live?

- What profession do you want to have?

- Who in this class (plays baseball, likes cats, etc.)?

- If you could go anywhere, where would it be?

Touch Red

Objectives: Practice colors while moving around the classroom.

Materials: A room with many different-colored things in it

Activity Directions and Preparation Hints

This is a simple but fun way to practice colors. Ask students to stand up. Give them the command "Touch red." They must move around the room and find something red to touch. Continue with other colors. This activity also works well with shapes. If you have competitive students, play it elimination style. No more than one student can touch an object of the color you called at the same time. If a student cannot find something of that color to touch, he or she has to sit out. Make the activity more challenging by adding an additional descriptor. For example, touch something soft and red, touch something shiny and white, and so on.

Two Truths and a Lie

Objectives: Write true and false statements about oneself.

Materials: Blank sheet of paper

Activity Directions and Preparation Hints

This is a good *get-to-know-you* activity. Have students take a few minutes to think about who they are and things they have done. Direct them to think about things they did when they were younger as well. Now, ask students to think about and write down two true statements and one false one about themselves. Tell students to make their lie believable and to pick two of the most outrageous truths about themselves.

Applications and Modifications

Use this simply as a get-to-know-you activity, or extend it. For more advanced levels, when the students present their statements, direct the audience to try to call the presenters' bluffs. Tell students they can drill the presenter by asking questions, such as when, with whom, where, and so on, about the statements. Ask students to write about one or both of the true statements they made and discuss them in the target language as a weekly journal topic. Allow students to choose to write about the false statement if they want to make a persuasive argument about why it is true or about how they would like for it to be true. Have students present their pieces to the class, share them with a partner, or just turn them in to you.

Walk-Around Activities

Objectives: Ask and answer questions about any topic while moving around the classroom.

Materials: Walk-Around Activity Template (Figure 6.5)

Activity Directions and Preparation Hints

Walk-around activities have multiple uses and allow students to get out of their seats to collect information from their classmates. Use this activity as an icebreaker, practice, or review activity. A walk-around activity worksheet can have various formats, including a table. Write questions in individual cells of the table. The student with the worksheet moves throughout the classroom, asking other students the question and recording their response.

Figure 6.5 Walk-Around Activity Template

© Activities, Games, and Assessment Strategies for the World Language Classroom, Amy Buttner Zimmer, Taylor & Francis

Applications and Modifications

Walk-around activities provide a venue for practicing vocabulary, grammar, culture, or content-related topics (see the following variations of the activity).

Application 1: Icebreaker Activity

Materials: Walk-Around Activity Template (see Figure 6.5)

Use the activity as an icebreaker at the beginning of the year, using a "Find someone who . . ." format. Sample questions might be to find someone who has been to Mexico, likes to golf, has a poodle, likes to eat pizza for breakfast, knows a Spanish greeting, doesn't like liver, and so forth. The odder and more interesting the questions, the better; those will get kids more interested in the activity and promote more conversation. Write each statement in a cell of the walk-around activity template. During the activity, students should record the name of the student to whom the statement applies in the cell.

Application 2: Teacher-Created Activity

Materials: Walk-Around Activity Template (see Figure 6.5)

Prepare by writing a question in each cell of the Walk-Around Activity Template (see Figure 6.5). Direct students to walk around the room and ask each other all the questions in their table. Ask the students to record the answer they are given in the same table cell as the question asked. Depending on the activity, you may want also want them to record who answered the question. As a follow-up to the activity, chart the information the students collected on the board and ask more questions about the results. Use this to practice questioning and answering questions in the target language, or apply it to vocabulary, grammar, content, or cultural topics that you would like students to practice.

Application 3: Student-Written Questions

Materials: Blank sheet of paper or 3×3 table

Involve students more creatively by asking them to write their own questions. Provide them with a nine-square table or ask them to fold a piece of paper so it has nine squares. Direct them to write nine questions, one in each square, leaving space for an answer. Check their questions for accuracy and then have them circulate through the room, asking their questions and recording their classmates' answers.

Application 4: Icebreaker Bingo Game

Materials: Walk-Around Activity Template (see Figure 6.5)

Do a walk-around activity that works as an icebreaker and a bingo game. This activity works well as name bingo at the beginning of the year. Use the "Find someone who" format or any other, and have students write down the name of the person who answered the question on the board. Play bingo using the students' names. Use the class seating chart as the way to call out a student's name for the game or an index card with his or her name on it.

Application 5: Key Questions Bingo Game

Materials: Walk-Around Activity Template (see Figure 6.5)

Prepare for this game by determining the questions you would like students to answer. For example, type in the two questions (*What time is it?* and *What is the weather like?*) throughout the board, one question in each cell, until you have filled the entire board. Prepare various answers to those questions, and write each one on a separate index card. Make sure you have the same number of answer cards as question cards for each of the two questions. To begin, pass out the bingo boards and one index card answer to each student. Direct students to go around the room, asking the questions on their bingo board to their classmates. If a student asks, "What time is it?" and the responding student has a weather expression, he or she should reply, "I don't know." The questioning student then asks the question, "What's the weather like?" Now the responding student can state the weather expression on his or her card. The questioning student should draw a picture of the weather on his or her board in a weather question box. For time expressions, the students should write in the numerical form of the time, such as 1:30 p.m. Once students have finished filling in their bingo board, collect the index cards with the answers from them and ask students to return to their seats. Pass out bingo markers and begin calling the game. Use the index cards with the answers as your calling cards.

Sample Topics:

- School supplies

- Food

- Questions with the key question words

- Yes or no questions

- Questions in the past tense

- Questions about Costa Rica after the students just researched it

- Questions about things students do and don't like to do

What Is It?

Objectives: Ask and respond to questions about an item.

Materials: Objects or pictures of objects you would like to teach or review

Activity Directions and Preparation Hints

Prepare by collecting objects or pictures of objects you would like to teach or review. Sit in a circle with your students, and model the game for the students using the following sequence:

The student next to you asks, "What is it?"

You respond by stating the name of the object.

The same student then asks, "Is it for me?"

You respond, "Yes, it's for you."

Continue the activity by passing the object/picture to the student. The sequence starts over with the next student.

Applications and Modifications

This activity works best with vocabulary items for which you have objects or pictures. Throw in a funny object, like a rubber chicken or plastic spider, to make the activity livelier. Once you have completed the activity, turn it into a writing activity by putting the objects on the table and asking students to write sentences, questions, a paragraph, or a dialogue that integrates as many words from the activity as they can. Differentiate by asking more advanced students to write a dialogue or paragraph, while more novice students work on sentences or questions.

Modification 1: Randomized Object Toss

Materials: Vocabulary objects

Instead of passing the objects around the circle in order, toss them across the circle randomly. This keeps students alert because they won't know when the object is coming to them.

Modification 2: Add More Objects

Materials: Vocabulary objects

Modify this activity once the students are comfortable with its basic format by adding in more objects one by one. See how long students can keep the activity going before the students or the objects get confused.

Sample Topics:

- Farm animals (use stuffed animals if you have them)
- School supplies
- Clothing
- Personal hygiene items
- Forms of transportation
- Colors
- Shapes
- Food items (use plastic ones if you have them)

Zoo Animals

Objectives: Identify an animal by the noise it makes.

Materials: Slips of paper, each with one animal name written on it

Activity Directions and Preparation Hints

This game can serve as an icebreaker activity as well as a way to review animals. Type a list of the names of various animals. Repeat each animal three times. Make sure to have enough slips for all your students. Pass out the name of an animal to each student. Instruct them to stand up, close their eyes, and start making the noise of their animal. They need to listen for others making that noise and carefully make their way toward them without opening their eyes. Once all students think they have found their group, they can open their eyes. Students in each group should say the name of their animal and double-check. Use this as a way to group students for a subsequent activity.

Sample Topics:

- Noises associated with professions (carpenter, plumber, teacher, secretary, nurse)

- Noises associated with places (kitchen, garage, zoo, subway, airport)

- Noises made by various forms of transportation

- Noises made by kitchen or home appliances

7

Games

Activity & Brief Description	Page	Application Areas				Type of Communication	
		VO	GR	CO	CU	Oral	Written
20 Questions One student goes into the hallway while other students hide an item. The returning student can ask up to 20 yes or no questions to find the object.	116	•	•			•	
Apples to Apples Prepare stacks of adjective and noun cards. Students play in small groups by selecting five noun cards. One student is the judge for each round and selects an adjective card. Other students must decide which of their nouns best matches the adjective. The judge decides which is the best and awards one point to the person who put in the noun card they liked best.	117	•		•	•	•	•
Around the World Students compete against other students one-on-one to identify vocabulary words. The winning student continues to compete against other students by going down the rows and challenging the next student.	118	•	•	•	•	•	
Battleship This is played just like the regular battleship game, except the board is on paper and marked with pencil. The student tries to guess the location of the opponent's ships by using coordinates. The first to find and sink all of their opponent's ships wins.	119	•	•			•	•
Bingo Students draw pictures in each space of a 5×5 grid. The teacher calls out the word in the target language. When students get five in a row, in the target language they call, "Bingo!"	119	•	•	•	•		
Board Games Find games in the target language, make your own, or have students design them so you can play them in class.	122	•	•	•	•	•	•

Activity & Brief Description	Page	Application Areas				Type of Communication	
		VO	GR	CO	CU	Oral	Written
Board Races Divide students into teams of five or six students. Students must take turns running to the board and writing up verb conjugations, vocabulary, and so forth. Points are awarded to teams based on the place they finish in and if the answers are correct.	124	•	•	•	•		•
Buzz Practice numbers with this game. Students count around the class and have to say, "Buzz!" when they hit a multiple of seven.	125	•				•	
Can You Say It? Students work in teams to pronounce unfamiliar words written on the board.	125	•	•	•	•	•	•
Card Stack Challenge Create three stacks of cards. Each stack represents a different part of speech. Students must work in teams to form a sentence with the word on each of the three cards they pick up.	126	•	•	•	•	•	•
Casino The teacher prepares a set of questions relevant to the topic of review. Students work individually and place bets on whether they will get the next question right before knowing what the question is.	127	•	•	•	•	•	•
Category Tag Students play tag but must say a word from a particular category of vocabulary to be *unfrozen*.	129	•		•	•	•	
Charades Students act out a word or situation that you provide. The audience guesses in the target language before time runs out. Play as a class, with two teams, or in small groups.	129	•	•		•	•	
Circumlocution Game Students divide into teams. One student describes a word to a teammate using circumlocution to guess it and earn a point for the team.	131	•	•	•	•	•	
College Quiz Bowl Students divide into two teams. The teacher asks questions of the teams. The first person to raise a hand can answer to earn a point for his or her team.	132	•	•	•	•	•	

Games

Activity & Brief Description	Page	Application Areas				Type of Communication	
		VO	GR	CO	CU	Oral	Written
Connect Four Students play in teams or pairs. Using a grid patterned after the game Connect Four, students must answer a question that combines an element from a row and one from a column. A correct answer allows the team to mark the meeting spot of the coordinates on the grid. Students try to get four correct in a row while blocking the other team.	133	•	•			•	
Continuation Students form a circle and are each given a verb or other vocabulary card. The students first show each other their verbs. The round begins with one student making a statement that includes a verb as well as the verb of another student. Continue until students can no longer think of the verbs of other students in the circle or play elimination style.	133	•	•			•	
Dress Up! In this game, students must put on the clothing they are given from a prop box by a member of the opposing team. The student also needs to state what he or she is wearing.	135	•	•			•	•
Five Divide the class into two teams. The object of this game is to score points by providing the correct answer to the question. Five students on each team go in a row, unless an incorrect answer is given. Students score one point for their team for each five people who give a correct response. If a student gives an incorrect response, it goes to the other team for a two-point steal. Cheating results in an opportunity to steal as well.	136	•	•	•	•	•	
The Flyswatter Game Write the vocabulary you would like to practice (or put pictures of it up) on the board or project it. Students form two teams. One student from each team is given a flyswatter. The teacher says the word in the target language if playing with pictures. The student who *swats* the picture first wins the point for the round.	137	•	•	•	•		•

Activity & Brief Description	Page	Application Areas				Type of Communication	
		VO	GR	CO	CU	Oral	Written
Go Fish Use the same matching cards you made for Concentration to play Go Fish. Students each take five to seven cards and take turns asking if an opponent has the match to a card he or she has in hand. If so, the opponent must hand over the card. If not, the opponent tells the other player to "Go Fish" and takes another card from the stack. The student who makes the most pairs wins.	138	•	•	•	•	•	
The Guessing Game Divide students into two teams, sending one player from each team into the hall. The rest of the class decides an object the hallway students will need to guess by asking questions about the object's uses.	140	•	•			•	
Hot Potato Sentences Students form a circle. The student with the ball begins by saying the first word of a sentence and passes the ball to the next person, who restates the previous word and adds a new one. Continue until the sentence can be no longer and then start a new one.	141	•	•			•	•
Label It in Time Students label a picture of an object or action with its corresponding word in the target language.	142	•	•	•	•		•
Off to the Races! Students divide into two teams. They will take turns answering questions from the teacher. All teammates should write down an answer on a whiteboard and confer to determine the best one. If the question is answered correctly, the team can move one space on the racetrack. The goal is to be the first to the finish line.	144	•	•	•	•	•	•
Oh No! After dividing into two teams, students answer questions posed by the teacher on any review topic. All students write down an answer on a whiteboard and confer, and then the team leader presents the best answer. Students receive points per round for correct responses.	144	•	•	•	•	•	•

Activity & Brief Description	Page	Application Areas				Type of Communication	
		VO	GR	CO	CU	Oral	Written
Pass It Up! Students are split in teams by rows. Pick a topic to review and give students the answers on a set of cards. Students work together to choose the correct answer that they then pass to the front of the row.	145	•	•	•	•	•	•
Pictionary Students take turns drawing a vocabulary word for the members of their team to guess.	145	•	•	•	•	•	
Presents Students brainstorm and create a set of index cards with possible gifts and a set with what someone likes to do. The class is divided into four teams and each student is given a gift index card. The teacher reads the person's description, and the students try to find the best match to the person's interests. Points are given to the team with the best match.	146	•	•	•		•	•
Ring a Word Call out a word in the students' native language; students from competing teams come to the board and try to be the first to find the equivalent in the target language and circle it. Write up two of each word and give students two different colored markers. Award points to the first to circle a word or to both teams for finding the word.	148	•	•	•	•		•
Row Races Create a row of students. This is their team. Each team gets a whiteboard. The teacher asks the first student to complete a task, such as writing a verb conjugation. The first student writes one conjugation and passes the board back through the row. Students keep adding the forms until the chart is complete. Students win points for correct answers.	149	•	•	•	•		•
Scattergories Once students are divided into teams, give them a letter of the alphabet and ask them to write as many words as they can that start with that letter. Students with more extensive vocabularies can be asked to provide words that start with that letter, using a specific category.	150	•		•	•		•

Activity & Brief Description	Page	Application Areas				Type of Communication	
		VO	GR	CO	CU	Oral	Written
Scrabble Students play a modification of the traditional scrabble game by forming words and writing them on a scrabble grid.	151	•	•	•	•		•
Simon Says Students practice commands and active verbs by doing what Simon says to do. However, if "Simon Says" is not said before the statement and students do the action, they must sit out for the rest of the round.	151	•				•	
Spud Students are each given a number (or other word) that they must remember. Students form a circle with one student in the middle, who is it. The student calls out a number and that person must run into the circle, catch the ball, and call out, "Spud!" All other students try to run away; but once "Spud!" is called, students must stop running and the person with the ball gets three strides to tag someone with the ball; otherwise, he or she gets a letter. Once a student gets all four letters in *spud*, they are out.	153	•	•	•	•	•	
Tic-Tac-Toe Divide students into pairs. Assign one student to be X and the other to be O. Each student in the pair writes a response to the teacher's question. If it is X's turn and X writes a correct response, student X can put an X in the tic-tac-toe grid. If X gets the answer wrong and O gives a correct answer, O can steal the point and put an O in the grid. Students play multiple games.	154	•	•	•	•		•
There's No Subject Students are given a sentence or question that is missing the subject. They need to figure out what the missing subject is to earn points for their team.	155	•		•	•	•	•
Verb War In pairs, students are given one stack of subject pronoun cards and one stack of verbs. Students place the stacks face down. Students pick up a card from each deck, and the first student to give the correct conjugation earns the point for that round.	155	•	•			•	•

Activity & Brief Description	Page	Application Areas				Type of Communication	
		VO	GR	CO	CU	Oral	Written
Vocabulary Puzzles Design a puzzle board by using the table feature in Microsoft Word. Write the English word on one side of the line, and write the target language word on the opposite side. Have students cut out the puzzle pieces and then put it back together by matching the English and target language words.	156	•	•	•	•	•	•
What Do You Remember? Make two lists of information for students to review. Each question has a different point value. Students divide into two teams and take turns quizzing each other. Students receive points according to the difficulty of the question they answer.	159	•	•	•	•	•	•
What's in the Bag? Put objects in a bag that you would like students to identify or describe. Students take turns putting their hand in the bag and guessing what is inside.	159	•	•	•	•	•	•
Word Race Game Give students various letters of the alphabet. In teams, ask them to write as many words as they can, using those letters.	160	•					•

VO = Vocabulary   GR = Grammar   CO = Content   CU = Culture

20 Questions

Objectives: Ask and answer yes and no questions; recall student names and common classroom items.

Materials: None; modified activities may require additional materials.

Activity Directions and Preparation Hints

Send one or two students out of the room while the class decides on a person or object in the classroom that the student(s) in the hall must figure out by asking yes or no questions. Help students begin guessing by modeling these two questions: Is it an object? Is it a person? You may want to require that they ask certain types of questions using adjectives, questions about the function of the object, or things the person likes to do. Students who guess the answer within the 20 questions are winners. Provide a prize if you wish.

Applications and Modifications

This is a good game to use when students are learning to form and answer yes or no questions in the target language. You can make it a little easier for the questioner by limiting students to choose items in the classroom that are in plain view or that have been recently studied.

Modification 1: Small-Group Play

Materials: Stack of cards with nouns for people, places, and things

Modify the game by having students play it in pairs. One pair of students plays against another pair. Provide each pair with a stack of cards that have words on them, representing people, places, or things. One student in the pair picks up a card. A student from the other pair has 1 minute to guess the word on the card by asking yes or no questions. Students earn a point for each correct guess. To save time, have each group of students make a set of cards for another group in the class. Encourage competitive students to make more challenging sets of cards by offering a small prize to the winners.

Modification 2: For Essential Question Practice

Materials: Two sets of questions, one for each partner; one answer key for each set of questions

Divide into groups of four, where pairs of two play against the other pair in the group. Provide students with a list of questions you want them to practice. Each pair needs a different set of questions. Also provide each pair with the answer key for their questions. Pair one asks pair two the first question on the list. The pair has 15 seconds to respond to the question. If they cannot provide the correct answer, the questioning team gets the point. If they can, they get the point for that round. If the answer given is incorrect, the questioning team should give the correct answer to the other team.

Sample Topics:

- School supplies and adjectives for size, color, physical traits, textures, etc.

- Family members and characteristics of living and nonliving things

- Shopping or nutrition units and related and unrelated descriptors

Apples to Apples

Objectives: Make noun-adjective associations; practice common nouns and adjectives; make decisions about the best noun-adjective combinations for a given situation.

Materials: One set of adjective cards, one set of noun cards

Activity Directions and Preparation Hints

Prepare one set of adjective cards and one of nouns. It is easiest if you color-code them so the adjective cards are one color and the nouns another. An efficient way to prepare the cards is by creating a table and typing an adjective into each cell. You can also use the Game Cards template included with the book. Print all the adjective cards on one color of cardstock and then cut them out. Do the same for the nouns.

To play, form a group of three to eight players. Give students the cards and direct them to leave the adjective cards on the table. Students take turns being the judge. The student judge cannot participate in that round. The judge for the first round begins by dealing out five noun cards to each player. The judge then flips over a card from the adjective stack. The players then pick the best noun in their hand to match the adjective on the table. Each player puts down a noun. The judge chooses the best noun and awards a point and the adjective card to that person. The next round continues with the person to the judge's left becoming the new judge and dealing a new noun to each player. The game then continues as long as desired. The player with the most adjective cards at the end of the game wins.

Applications and Modifications

Although the grammatical application is somewhat limited by the structure of the game, the game can be adapted to use subjects and infinitives as the two categories. In this case, students receive the subject cards and the judge turns over the infinitive cards. Add in writing practice by challenging students to create the funniest sentence using both of their words. Instead of turning in the subject card, the students turn in their sentences to the judge. The judge awards points based on which sentence is the funniest and gives the winner the infinitive card. Make a postgame writing extension by asking the students to pick their favorite funny sentence and include it in a paragraph or short story.

Sample Topics:

- Noun-adjective pairings with professions and characteristic adjectives

- Noun-adjective pairings with objects and adjectives that describe the size, age, quality, the way the object feels, and so on

- Subject-infinitive combinations using verbs in a particular tense and a variety of interesting subjects

Around the World

Objectives: Provide a response to a question in the game.

Materials: Flashcards

Activity Directions and Preparation Hints

No special setup is needed for this game. Have the first student in a row stand next to the student seated behind him or her. Show a flashcard, and the first of the two people to answer the question wins the round. If the person standing wins, they move back to stand next to the person seated behind the person who lost the round. If the seated person wins, he or she stands up and takes the place of the person who was standing. The standing person sits down in that spot. To win, the student must make it all the way around the classroom and back to where he or she started. This is a great time-filler activity for those extra few minutes at the end of the hour. It is also another way to make use of the flashcards you made for the lesson.

Applications and Modifications

Practice vocabulary, grammatical, content-based, or cultural topics with this game. Any information that can be put on a flashcard and requires a short answer works well for this game.

Sample Topics:

- Any vocabulary

- Questions in the target language

- Artist and their work

- Math problems to practice numbers

- Cultural celebration questions

- Verb conjugation practice by stating or showing a subject and a verb

Battleship

Objectives: Recall and use vocabulary; conjugate verbs using selected subjects and verbs; practice noun-adjective agreement; combine subjects and predicates; combine possessive adjectives and nouns.

Materials: Battleship Board (Figure 7.1)

Activity Directions and Preparation Hints

Battleship is played with the objective of sinking the opponent's ship. Each student has a paper grid on which to hide four ships of varying sizes. A student takes turns trying to guess the location of the opponent's ships using the coordinates on the grid.

Applications and Modifications

Use the game to review grammatical topics. For example, use the left column of the grid for subject pronouns and the top row for infinitives. To guess, the student must correctly conjugate the verb corresponding to the coordinate. To control for accuracy, the teacher can move about the room listening and assisting students, as well as having the students track their guesses and those of their partner in writing beneath the grid (see, e.g., Figure 7.1). The game can also be used for any vocabulary topic. Students can use discrete vocabulary, like colors and numbers, or it can be more complex by combining weather and months to form a sentence, such as, "The weather is nice in January."

Sample Topics:

- Subjects and verbs (regular, irregular, reflexives, stem-changers, etc.)

- Possessive adjectives and objects

- Noun/adjective agreement

- Subjects and predicates of sentences

- Colors and numbers

- Weather and months

Bingo

Objectives: Match a vocabulary word heard in the target language with its picture; match a vocabulary word heard in English with a word written in the target language; find a picture or word in the target language from a spoken context clue.

Materials: Bingo board (Figure 7.2)

RESOURCES

	To wake up early	To shower	To brush one's hair	To eat breakfast	To go to school	To do homework	To eat supper	To watch television	To go to bed	To sleep
I										
You										
He										
She										
You (formal)										
The family										
The cat										
We										
They										
You all										

Submarine   Destroyer   Aircraft Carrier   Battleship

Write the guesses you and your partner made in the spaces provided.

My Guesses

1. _____
2. _____
3. _____
4. _____
5. _____
6. _____
7. _____
8. _____

My Partner's Guesses

1. _____
2. _____
3. _____
4. _____
5. _____
6. _____
7. _____
8. _____

Figure 7.1 Battleship Board

RESOURCES

		Free Space		

Figure 7.2 Bingo Board

© *Activities, Games, and Assessment Strategies for the World Language Classroom*, Amy Buttner Zimmer, Taylor & Francis

Activity Directions and Preparation Hints

This is another old favorite in world language classrooms. Traditional bingo boards have *bingo* spelled out at the top of each column and have one number in each of the 25 squares that make up the bingo grid. Students listen for the number in the target language and put a chip on the square of the number they hear. Students must get five in a row vertically, horizontally, or diagonally. Also they can play to get four corners or to cover the whole board.

Applications and Modifications

Bingo is a useful game to review vocabulary, content-based, cultural, and some grammatical topics. Provide students with premade Bingo boards or use the ideas that follow to have them make their own.

Modification 1: Student-Drawn Boards

Materials: Blank 5 × 5 grid, bingo chips

Give students a blank 5 × 5 grid. Review vocabulary and have them make their own bingo board at the same time. Say the word you would like them to illustrate in one square on their grid. Remind students to draw their illustrations randomly on the board to avoid making the same card as someone else. Allow them a brief period of time to illustrate the word and continue until the students have drawn all the words. As an alternative, have the students draw the pictures for their game board at home as a homework assignment. Pass out the bingo chips and they are ready to play. If you don't have bingo chips, students can use a symbol that they mark on their board to indicate what was called. They can erase it between rounds or just use a different symbol. Call the words using flashcards you already have for the vocabulary you have been teaching or cards you write up for the game. Another option is to use an extra vocabulary sheet you have from the unit and draw a symbol next to the word you call. Change the symbol for each round and use the sheet multiple times.

Modification 2: Walk-Around Oral Questioning Practice and Bingo

Materials: Blank 5 × 5 grid

This works great at the beginning of the year as a get-to-know you activity. Students take their boards and walk around the room, asking other students their name in the target language. Students record the names of the other students, and that becomes the source for the bingo game. If you use the 3 × 5 index cards for student information and name cards, these can be your source for calling the game. A class attendance list can also be used by putting a mark after the name of the student you call. You can use different symbols for each round to keep the names you have called straight.

Board Games

Objectives: Make and play board games to practice oral and written language.

Materials: Materials vary based on the option you choose. You may need the following:

- Board games from the target culture
- Paper (8½ × 11 or legal size)
- Cardstock

- Markers

- Crayons

- Laminator

- Game cards

- Game tokens

- A board game template found from an online search. (Also look in the images that come up in the search engine you use. Consider also using the browser set to the language of your target language country for more options.)

Activity Directions and Preparation Hints

The board games category can be interpreted in different ways. The first way is for you to search out board games in the target language that students can play after tests or on special game days. Another way to do board games is for you or the students to design them based on popular existing games or to create new ones. If you or the students design one, make a nice blackline master first. From there you can get copies of it, students can color them in, and then you can have them laminated. Try using legal-size paper to get a bigger game board or putting two 8½ × 11 sheets together. For a heavier game board, make the copies on cardstock. This might be a fun individual or group project, especially for your artistic students. For the game cards, create a table in a word processing program to get uniformly sized cards and have students type one question in each cell. Print them on different colors of cardstock to distinguish different types of questions if needed. For example, make grammar-related questions on green cards and vocabulary on red.

Applications and Modifications

Student- or teacher-made board games can be used as a review of any vocabulary, grammatical, content-based, or cultural information. If the students make them, ask them to pick the essential topics and vocabulary from the unit they are studying and incorporate them into a game other students can play to review. Give them specific guidelines of what you are looking for in the game, and reinforce the importance of spelling things correctly. Use the games again later in the year to review topics from previous lessons. This type of activity could also make a good sub plan, provided that there are clear directions and guidelines.

Sample Game Topics:

1. Review basic topics: numbers, colors, days of the week, weather, time, telling the date, and basic questions (What is your name? How are you?).

2. Review topics and verbs related to school: school supplies, people who work there, classes, necessary verbs and grammar for talking about school, time, ordinal numbers, and so forth.

3. After completing a unit on Spain, use the game to review the features you highlighted in your unit: its architecture and well-known places, famous people (artists, architects, musicians, leaders, scientists, etc.), geography and regions, the different languages spoken, language characteristics, related vocabulary and grammar, and so on.

4. After reading a novel, have students make a game that identifies main characters and their characteristics, themes of the novel, major events, important new vocabulary learned, and so forth.

Board Races

Objectives: Review verb conjugations in a team game format as well as vocabulary or other information from a particular category.

Materials: Whiteboard, dry-erase markers

Activity Directions and Preparation Hints

This game gets students out of their desks and moving while practicing a topic of your choice. Begin by creating teams of five or six students. Assign each team a number and designate a spot on the whiteboard for each group. Groups could also use individual whiteboards that they run up to you. Using the example of verb conjugation practice, state a verb and the tense in which you would like the verb to be conjugated. When you tell students to begin, one student from each team runs to the board and writes down the first-person singular conjugation. They then run back to their teams and pass the marker, and the next two players run to the board to write the second-person singular form. Play until the verb has been completely conjugated. Allow students to fix their teammates' errors if they find them before the round finishes. Choose a judge to track the order in which teams finish. Once all teams are done, ask students to look at all the responses on the board. Start with the team that finished first. Ask all students to look for any errors. If there are any, that team is disqualified and wins no points. Continue this brief evaluation process for each team. Students are motivated to look critically at the answers on the board because they can prevent other teams from getting points. Decide if you want to award more points for the first team with all the correct answers or if all teams that are correct receive the same amount. Continue the game through various rounds.

Applications and Modifications

Board races work best when you have a single topic that requires multiple answers to complete the task, such as verb conjugations. Generally, there should be one response for each person on the team to write, so make sure to divide into teams accordingly. Typically five or six students on a team works out the best.

Sample Topics:

- Verb conjugations in any tense
- Possessive adjectives and nouns
- Verb conjugations
- Countries and capitals of Europe
- Important characters from a work of fiction students are reading and their characteristics, roles in the novel, and so forth
- Items found in a kitchen, living room, and so on; pick a different room for each round
- Items found in specific sections of a department store
- Key contributions of selected historical figures

Buzz

Objectives: Practice numbers orally.

Materials: None

Activity Directions and Preparation Hints

This is a fun game to take the monotony out of practicing numbers. Begin by having students form a circle. They can sit or stand. The students begin counting from 1 while passing a ball around the circle. The students must say, "Buzz!" ("¡Epa!" is a fun expression for Spanish) when the number reaches 7. All numbers with 7 in them (7, 17, 27, etc.) must be replaced with the word *buzz.* Make it more complicated by making students replace multiples of 7 with "Buzz" as well.

Can You Say It?

Objectives: Apply pronunciation rules to new words in a competition; recall old vocabulary words and learn new ones.

Materials: Whiteboard, dry-erase marker

Activity Directions and Preparation Hints

This game practices word identification and pronunciation. Divide the class into two teams or have the class play against the teacher. Write a word or sentence on the board. If the team can correctly translate and pronounce it, they get a point. If incorrect, the other team gets a chance to translate and pronounce the word to steal the round for double points.

Applications and Modifications

This is a good game to play with introductory levels to help them find patterns in pronunciation and draw attention to sound symbol associations of the language to help them with spelling.

Modification 1: Student-Chosen Words

Materials: Blank sheet of paper, vocabulary lists (optional), dictionaries (optional)

Before beginning the game, give the teams a few minutes to create a list of words that they challenge the other team to pronounce. Allow students to use their vocabulary lists and dictionaries. Then ask each team to submit the list to you.

Modification 2: Adding Circumlocution

Materials: Blank sheet of paper, vocabulary lists (optional), dictionaries (optional)

To modify this to be more challenging, ask upper-level students to pronounce the word correctly and use circumlocution to describe the word or provide its definition.

Games

Sample Topics:

- Any vocabulary topics, especially ones that might have difficult spellings or sound combinations on which you would like to focus students' attention

- For advanced levels, more complex words to practice circumlocution, as well as pronunciation

- A list of words chosen because of a particular letter combination

Card Stack Challenge

Objectives: Conjugate verbs; form sentences; use prepositions in a phrase or sentence; correctly order nouns and adjectives; apply agreement rules.

Materials: Sets of prepared or blank game cards, whiteboard, dry-erase markers

Activity Directions and Preparation Hints

Make a stack of cards with subjects, verbs in their infinitive form, and objects. The teacher can prepare this ahead of time or brainstorm them with the students and have volunteers in the class write them down as the teacher writes them up on the board. Different groups of students also can write them for other student groups in the class. Color-code the card stacks with subjects as one color, verbs another, and objects a third color. Use colored index cards or cardstock cut down to the size you would like. To play, divide the class into two teams; select two judges and one scorekeeper who do not play on a team. The judges take turns selecting a card from each stack. A representative from each team waits at the front white board. The judges read the three words out loud. The judges should block the students from looking at each other's work to avoid copying. The students have 30 seconds to write the most original and longest sentence they can that includes the three words. The judges award points for length of the sentence, giving one point per word. The judges also award points for creativity. One possibility for awarding creativity points is to give the judges a total of five points to award as they see fit. If the students write the same sentence, nobody gets points. Give the judges 30 seconds to decide the points to award, and then move on to the next round.

Applications and Modifications

This game practices both grammar and vocabulary. Incorporate content and culture on a basic level by incorporating them into the subjects and objects.

Modification 1: Randomly Chosen Answers

Materials: Personal whiteboards, dry-erase markers

Use the preceding rules with one exception. Each student on a team has a whiteboard and writes a sentence for the words given. Have a judge call on a random student from each team to share the sentence. Judge as in the original rules.

Modification 2: Pair Up!

Materials: Personal whiteboards, dry-erase markers

Play with the same rules as in the original game with one exception. Divide the class into teams, and then pair up students from rival teams so they are seated next to each other. The judges read the three words, and the students each write a sentence. When finished, they read each other's answers and check for accuracy. Each student receives points based on the length of the response. If the answer is not accurate, no points are awarded. In this version you may want to have the students hold up the boards so you can do a visual check or circulate around the room to check any answer that a partner questions. Students can either play against their partner or play for a total amount of points to be added to their team score.

Modification 3: Group of Three

Materials: One set of cards for groups of three, personal whiteboards, dry-erase markers

Play this version with a group of three students. Each student picks up a different card, and together they write a sentence that uses all three words. Practice a variety of verb tenses with this activity, adjusting for the student level. If each group of students makes a set of cards for another group, this activity can be done as a timed activity, where students must keep picking from the stack of cards to make as many grammatically correct sentences as possible. Vary the grammar practiced by changing the card stacks slightly. Practice direct object pronouns by asking the students to write the sentence changing the object to a direct object pronoun. Make the sentences more complex by asking the students to not just use the three words from the stacks but to add a prepositional phrase, adjective, and so forth.

Sample Topics:

- Practice verb conjugation in any tense.

- Practice noun-adjective agreement.

- Determine if sentences are logical after they have been formed by using a mix of cards that will yield both logical and illogical sentences.

Casino

Objectives: Review topics from class, competing individually against other classmates to earn points.

Materials: Casino Template (Figure 7.3)

Activity Directions and Preparation Hints

This game works well for reviewing any information you would like. It can make what might be a not so interesting review of vocabulary via flashcards into an intense competition without requiring any additional preparation. Pass out the game template (see Figure 7.3) or scratch paper to students, and ask them to divide the paper into columns: bets, answers, winnings, and losses. Tell students how much money they have for their initial bet and the currency you are using. You can make the amount the same for each student or you can vary the amounts. Before you ask or show the first question, students must write in the amount they want to bet for that round. They may not bet more than they have! Ask the question and have students record the answer in the answer column. When students finish, show or tell the students the correct answer. Students who are correct should add their winnings to their original amount; students who lost the bet should subtract. Ask the students to convert the unit of currency you used to dollars before completing the game. If you are giving a

Bets	Answers	Winnings	Losses
Total Losses			
Total Winnings			
Grand Total			

Figure 7.3 Casino Template

prize to the student with the most money at the end of the game, you may want to ensure honest playing by pairing students up so that they check each other's answers and bets as the game progresses. If students run out of money, you can opt to give them a loan of a few euros, pesos, etc. Or you can tell them they can start betting other things that are "theirs." Some students get really into this one and start betting anything from pencils to siblings.

Category Tag

Objectives: Review vocabulary in categories.

Materials: None

Activity Directions and Preparation Hints

Use this game to practice vocabulary recall. Begin by choosing a category of words. Some possibilities include food, clothing, and weather. Make sure that students have learned the vocabulary well enough to be able to produce the words in the target language with ease. You need some open space for this activity, as students will be playing a game of tag. You can begin as the *tagger* or choose a student to be *it*. If students are tagged, they must say a word from the chosen category or they have to be frozen for the round. Students cannot repeat a word from the category. If they do and the tagger catches them doing it, they are automatically frozen.

Applications and Modifications

Vary the rounds by changing categories of words. Allow students to become unfrozen if they can say a word from the category to the student who *unfreezes* them. Play the game entirely in the target language by teaching the students a few key phrases, such as, "Help me," "Over here," and "Save me!" Students also can be automatically frozen by you or the tagger if they are heard speaking in English.

Sample Topics:

- Professions

- Animals

- Names of . . . (Spanish/French, etc.) cities/places in the . . . (United States, Canada, etc.)

- Things in a . . . (school, museum, library, restaurant, etc.)

- Things found in nature

- Items that start with the letter "S"

Charades

Objectives: Take turns acting out vocabulary for classmates to guess in the target language.

Materials: List of vocabulary words or flashcards

Activity Directions and Preparation Hints

This well-known game is great for practicing vocabulary that can be acted out. Divide students into two teams. Have the first student from one team come to the front of the room. Show the student a word from your set of flashcards or vocabulary list. The student then has up to 1 minute to act out the word so teammates can guess. Have students from the team raise their hand or stand up when they know the answer. Call on a student to answer. If an incorrect answer is given, you may choose to offer the option of guessing the word to the other team to *steal* the points.

Applications and Modifications

This game works best with words that can be acted out with relative ease. It works great with action verbs, commands, and various nouns. With enough context it can work with some cultural and content-based vocabulary.

Modification 1: Small-Group Charades

Materials: List of vocabulary words or flashcards

Divide students up into groups of seven. In each group one student is in charge of moderating the game and choosing the words that each group of three takes turns acting out for the other trio. Points are awarded when the student successfully acts out the word so the rest of his or her group can guess. Rotate turns between the two teams.

Modification 2: The Hot Seat

Materials: List of vocabulary words or flashcards

A student volunteers to act out the vocabulary words. The students in the audience raise their hand to tell the volunteer what to act out. The audience's goal is to stump the volunteer so he or she tries to find more challenging words. If you are teaching clothes and have a prop box, students can tell the student in the *hot seat* what clothes to put on. The more eclectic the collection of clothes you have, the better! Decide how many words the volunteer in the hot seat must perform correctly to win a small prize.

Writing Activity Extension

Materials: Blank piece of paper

Ask students to write down the things that they saw acted out in the past tense and the name of the student who acted them out. They can jot down the name of the person and the verb while the game is going on to help them remember who did what.

Sample Topics:

- Animals

- Sports

- Classroom commands

- Action verbs

- Professions

- Famous people

- Transportation

Circumlocution Game

Objectives: Use circumlocution to describe a word so a teammate can guess what it is.

Materials: List of vocabulary words or flashcards

Activity Directions and Preparation Hints

In this game students practice the skill of circumlocution. Create two teams of students. One student from each team stands in front of the classroom, facing away from the board. Write or draw a word on the board behind the students. A student from one of the teams in the audience has to stand up and explain the word on the board to the contestants so they can guess what it is. The explaining students cannot say the word, and nor can the audience. For example, if the word is *cookies*, the describing student might say, "You give them to Santa on Christmas, they have chocolate in them, they are round, you bake them in an oven," and so forth. The student who guesses the word first wins the point for the team. Create a reasonable time limit for each round. New students should come to the board from each team every round, and the student who describes the word should rotate between the two teams.

Applications and Modifications

This game works well to practice describing people, places, things, and actions.

Modification 1: Small Groups

Materials: List of vocabulary words

This game is most effective when played in smaller groups because it gives more students the opportunity to participate. Create groups of seven students. One student is the list master and judge. The remaining six students divide into groups of three. The list master has the list of words you would like the students to describe with circumlocution. One possible way to direct the game is to have one student describe the word to his or her other two teammates. The list master/judge keeps time for the round and records points. If the team guessing is unable to determine the correct answer within the time limit, the other team can take a guess for a steal. Steals are worth double points. The teams take turns until the time is up for the activity. The team with the most points wins.

Sample Topics:

- Professions

- Specific foods

- School supplies

- Clothing

- Household actions

- School-related verbs

College Quiz Bowl

Objectives: Review class material in a team format.

Materials: Prepared list of questions

Activity Directions and Preparation Hints

Begin by preparing a list of questions you would like students to answer. Provide students with the list of questions a couple of days before the game to promote review. Divide students into teams of three or four members. Have each team select a name of a college (sports team, company, car, etc.) they represent in the game. Ask a question and allow any team member to offer a response by first raising his or her hand; the first person to raise his or her hand can answer. Make this more exciting by giving out maracas, tambourines, and so on to the students. When they want to answer, they make a noise with their instrument. Teams score a point for each member's correct response.

Applications and Modifications

This game can be used to review vocabulary, grammar, content, or culture. Any style of question format from multiple choice to short answer works well with this game. Modify the game by having teams take turns answering the questions.

Modification 1: Two Teams and an Audience

Materials: Study guide with the questions used in the Quiz Bowl

Make two Quiz Bowl teams and have the rest of the students be part of the audience. Give the students in the audience a list of the questions being asked in the Quiz Bowl. As they hear the answers, they should write them down. Another option is to have them fill in the study guide ahead of time with their answers and make any corrections during the Quiz Bowl. Students participating in the Quiz Bowl can also have a study guide without answers, or you can give them one with answers filled in after the game if they need one.

Modification 2: Student-Written Quiz Bowl

Materials: Student questions for the Quiz Bowl, master list of questions, or study guide for the Quiz Bowl

In pairs or groups, have students write what they feel are the important questions they should review in the Quiz Bowl a couple of days ahead of time. You also may want to ask students to submit the answers to their questions. Students give the questions to you for use in the game. You then review the students' submissions to determine the best questions. Add in any of your own questions as you compile the master questions list.

Sample Topics:

- Questions about characters, plot, conflict, and so forth in one or various books
- Comparison of various artists and their work
- Specific questions about grammar
- Review of all essential questions for the year
- Review for a final exam

Connect Four

Objectives: Conjugate verbs in any tense chosen by the teacher.

Materials: Connect Four Grid (Figure 7.4), colored markers, empty game board (optional)

Activity Directions and Preparation Hints

Play this game as a class, in small groups, or in pairs. You need a game board that is six rows wide and five columns tall. Use Figure 7.4 for the game board or create your own. The object of the game is to be the first team to get four correct answers marked in a column, row, or diagonal line with their team's color. Students should strategize to block the other team from connecting four in a row. For whole-class play, divide students into two teams. Have a projected copy of the game board. Have two colors of markers, one color for each team. The students must start at the bottom of the grid and work their way up as if stacking building blocks. In the case of a game that practices verb conjugation, the first team reads a subject and a verb from the chart and then conjugates it. If the conjugation is correct, the teacher writes the conjugation in the corresponding space and in the team's color. The next team chooses their subject-verb combination as well and conjugates the verb. Decide whether the opposing team can steal the space if they can provide a correct answer when the first team loses their turn for giving an incorrect answer. To involve more students in the game, pass out individual whiteboards. Each student should write an answer down for the question being asked, even if it is not their team's turn.

Applications and Modifications

Use any vocabulary, grammar, content-based, or cultural topic that fits with a grid setup.

Modification 1: Pair or Group Play

For pair or small-group play, provide students with one empty game board on which they track their answers. You may also want to give them one board that has the answers so students can verify their answers. It works well in a small group game to have one student be the game leader and be in charge of verifying the students' answers for accuracy.

Sample Topics:

- Form basic yes and no questions with the subject and verb.

- Practice noun-adjective agreement with gender and number by putting a noun in the rows and an adjective in each of the columns.

- Practice possessive adjective and noun agreement.

- Form a sentence by putting a subject pronoun and an infinitive in the row and a place in the columns. Students have to conjugate the verb and connect the place to the sentence with a logical preposition.

Continuation

Objectives: Recall verbs and vocabulary and use them in a sentence orally.

Materials: Vocabulary flashcards

	To know	To believe	To drink	To write	To live	To put	To make	To see
I								
You								
Julia								
Marcos								
You (formal)								
We								
They								
You all								
Definition								

Figure 7.4 Connect Four Grid

Activity Directions and Preparation Hints

Use this game with any vocabulary. To play the game with verbs, you need flashcards with verbs written in their infinitive form. Choose a category of verbs you would like students to practice. Have students stand up and form a circle. Pass out one verb flashcard to each student. Give yourself a card as well and join in the circle. For at least the first round, allow students to show their cards to other students. As a challenge in a later round, you may ask students to cover the verb on their card. Start the game by saying a sentence with your verb, along with someone else's. Students must create a logical sentence using their word, another student's word, and any other vocabulary needed to connect the two—for example, "In the morning I get up and I eat breakfast." The person who has the phrase *to eat breakfast* on his or her card has to make up a new sentence quickly with his or her word and a new person's. As soon as students create a correct response, they can sit down. Once a student is seated, other students may no longer use that verb. If the student is not able to make a correct statement, he or she must remain standing and stay in the game. The last person standing begins the next round.

Applications and Modifications

Play this game using categories, such as verbs, nouns, vocabulary themes, and so on. You may choose to review a particular area or create a collection of very random words to give the students a fun challenge and review. Create more of a challenge by specifying a particular tense for students to use or just let students determine that naturally.

Sample Topics:

- Reflexive verbs
- Summer activities
- Family members and things they do together
- Chores at home
- School activities
- Sports and recreation
- Picnic vocabulary
- Selection of words not specific to any topic

Dress Up!

Objectives: Identify the name of the clothing they have been given to put on and create a complete sentence with the clothing item that includes a description of it.

Materials: Box of clothing for student use

Activity Directions and Preparation Hints

This game practices clothing items and you will need a bag of clothing for it. If you don't have a collection of clothing for the classroom, check rummage sales in the summer or see if any of your students' parents or staff at school are cleaning out closets and want to donate to your collection. Students form teams and select members to represent their team in the competition. One student from each team comes to the front of the room. The student competing in that round receives three items of clothing from the member of the opposing team. The competing student must put on the clothes, making statements such as, "This is my shirt" or "These are my pants." Change the statement to fit your language practice needs. The student can earn a point for each correct statement about the clothing item. They can earn an additional point per item if they correctly use an adjective in the statement. Once the competing student finishes, the student who chose the clothing from the opposing team becomes the contestant. Continue the game until students lose interest or you reach a predetermined number of points. If you want to record some of the segments in video, you could replay any funny ones or replay if you want to identify any grammatical points for discussion. If you are using a tablet or other recording device, it may be easiest to create separate short segments for each group. It could also make an entertaining addition to a class blog post. This activity might also be an entertaining picture opportunity, provided that students are fine with it.

Applications and Modifications

Modification 1: Audience Writes What They Hear

Materials: Blank sheet of paper

One way to further involve the audience is to ask them to record the statements made by their teammate or by both teams. If students write down the statements they hear, they stay more focused and you have some sentences to work with after the game. Here are three ideas on how to use the sentences after the game:

1. Ask the students to illustrate the statements.

2. Ask the students to check for errors in the statements that were made by the contestants and correct them.

3. Ask students in the audience to read a statement while another student finds the clothing described and holds it up.

Five

Objectives: Recall vocabulary words.

Materials: Flashcards

Activity Directions and Preparation Hints

This is a good filler game to play with any set of flashcards. Divide students into two or three teams. Show a flashcard for the student closest to you and ask for the meaning of the word. If the student answers correctly, the game continues on the student's side to the next person behind him or her in the row. To get a point, five students must respond with the correct answer. After one round, the turn automatically goes to the next team. Students must answer as individuals on the team. If someone from their team gets caught giving the responding student the answer, they lose their turn; the other team has the opportunity to steal for two points and they get the next turn. You can play the game where students can *phone a friend* on the team and ask for help once, as in the game show *Millionaire.* If the friend gives the correct answer, the team keeps their turn. If not, the other team can steal the question. Teammates may not be *called* more than once and may not indicate in any way if they know the answer.

The Flyswatter Game

Objectives: Match a word in the target language with a picture or a word in English.

Materials: Whiteboard with words or pictures on it, two or three flyswatters

Activity Directions and Preparation Hints

This game can be applied to any vocabulary, grammatical, cultural, or content-related topic. Divide students into two or three teams. Prepare for the game by writing words, approximately 12 to 20, or putting pictures of the words on the whiteboard ahead of time. Call up one student from each team to the front, and give each one a flyswatter. Call out the word in the target language if there is a picture or provide a context clue in the target language if students have a picture or have a target language word on the board. You can also work say the word in English if the target language word is on the board. The first student to *swat* the correct word wins a point for the team. Continue with the next round by having the winner of that round stay to take on a new challenger from the other team or by having both students sit and two new competitors replace them at the board.

Applications and Modifications

Modification 1: Pair Flyswatter

Materials: Flyswatter game sheet, colored pens

A modification of this game is to write the words or put the pictures on paper and make enough copies so there is one for each pair or group of three students. Then the pairs or groups of students compete to *swat* the word or picture first with their finger. Students can cross off the words with different colored pens to track points or write down their initials on the words they *swatted* first. This version of the game involves all students for the whole activity.

Extensions

Some extensions of this activity include asking the students to do the following:

A. Illustrate the words, sentences, or other concepts from the game.

B. Write sentences or a story using as many words from the game as possible.

C. Make up a song.

Sample Topics:

*   Food vocabulary

*   Items in the classroom

*   Action verbs

- Classroom expressions

- Verbs conjugated to various tenses or subject forms

- Famous artists (musicians, historical figures, paintings, places, etc.)

- Names of cultural celebrations

Go Fish!

Objectives: Match words in the target language with pictures or words in English.

Materials: Set of Go Fish Cards (Figure 7.5)

Activity Directions and Preparation Hints

This game is played like the traditional Go Fish game. You or your students need to make a set of cards (see Figure 7.5). The set should have a picture of a vocabulary word and a matching word or phrase in the target language. If no picture is available, use the English word. Type a word in one cell and insert a picture into the cell next to the word. Continue until you have enough cards. Print the cards and copy them onto a darker colored cardstock to avoid having the words and pictures show through the cards. Save time by having the students cut out the cards. To play, a student deals seven cards to each player. Students take turns asking each other for the item that they need to make a match. The student with the most pairs at the end of the game wins.

Applications and Modifications

Go Fish is a basic game that is good for pairs to practice vocabulary objects. It will work well if following the traditional *Do you have a . . .* question format. However, with a little bit of creativity this game can be stretched to practice different questions and verb tenses.

Modification 1: Asking Other Yes and No Questions

Materials: Set of Go Fish cards (see Figure 7.5)

Get beyond the *Do you have a . . .* question by setting up other questions students should ask. If the cards include sports, try using the question, "Do you play . . . ?" For clothing ask, "Do you buy (wear, like) . . . ?" Responding students give an affirmative answer if they have the object and a negative if they don't. Ask students to respond in complete sentences. Change the subject of the question to practice answering questions with other verb forms. For food vocabulary ask, "Does your mom buy . . . at the grocery store?" Ask the question, "Did you see . . . ?" to practice names of animals at the zoo, famous people, art, and more. One way to challenge beginning students would be to ask them to use direct object pronouns in their answer, instead of simply repeating back the object being asked about in the question. For example, respond to the question, "Did you eat my cookies?" with "Yes, I ate them."

Modification 2: Question Formation, Conjugation, and Verb Practice

Materials: Set of Go Fish cards (see Figure 7.5)

Create Go Fish cards that have verbs or verb phrases and corresponding pictures for the action. Practice the verb, question formation, and conjugations in a particular tense. Some questions require students to improvise a logical

Figure 7.5 Go Fish Cards

© *Activities, Games, and Assessment Strategies for the World Language Classroom*, Amy Buttner Zimmer, Taylor & Francis

response. Any negative response indicates that the student does not have the card. See the following examples and their responses:

1. Do you swim?

   a. Yes, I swim.

   b. No, I don't swim.

2. Does your family like to rent movies?

   a. Yes, we like to rent them.

   b. No, we don't like to rent them.

3. What does your brother buy?

   a. My brother buys video games.

   b. My brother doesn't buy anything.

4. Where did you go?

   a. I went to the movies.

   b. I didn't go anywhere.

A little creativity takes Go Fish to a higher level for more advanced students and will make it useful for practicing other types of questions.

Sample Topics:

- Food

- Items in a garage

- Sports equipment

- Questions that ask for information

- Yes and no questions

- Famous people

- Cultural celebrations

The Guessing Game

Objectives: Form questions to guess the name of a mystery object.

Materials: None; however, a vocabulary list or list of topics may be helpful.

Activity Directions and Preparation Hints

This game reviews vocabulary and formation of questions. It is also an excellent activity to practice asking a variety of questions and review previously learned vocabulary and language structures. Divide the class into teams. Send one person from each team into the hallway while the class picks an object from the designated vocabulary list for the students outside to guess. When the students return, they take turns asking questions of the group about the object, such as the following:

- "When do I use it?"

- "Where do I use it?"

- "Why do I use it?"

- "Can I eat it?"

- "Do I wear it?"

- "Would I want to give one to a friend?"

Either contestant may guess the word after asking a question when it is his or her turn. If the contestant guesses wrong, he or she loses a turn. You may want to put a limit on the number of questions each contestant may ask. Send new contestants to the hallway for each round. The team with the most correct answers wins.

Applications and Modifications

The game can be modified by sending only one student into the hallway at a time, so teams take turns earning points. Another possible modification is to divide the class into smaller groups and have teams within those groups play against one another. This modification allows for a greater number of students to participate at one time.

Sample Topics:

- School supplies

- Things you might find in your grandma's attic

- Items in the school cafeteria's kitchen

- Things you would pack in a suitcase to go to Paris in the spring

- Things and animals you find at the zoo

- Car parts

- Things you find at Disneyland

- Items you can find at a department store

Hot Potato Sentences

Objectives: Form sentences in a group word by word.

Materials: One soft ball for students to toss to one another

Activity Directions and Preparation Hints

In this game students practice sentence formation. Students form a circle and sit down, facing each other. The teacher begins with the ball, says one word, and passes the ball to the right. The student receiving the ball adds a word and passes the ball on as quickly as possible, as if it is hot. Because the game is *Hot Potato*, the idea is to keep the ball moving around the circle as fast as possible. The round stops when a student is no longer able to add to the sentence or when the teacher stops it because the sentence is no longer making sense.

Applications and Modifications

Modification 1: More Difficult Rules

Materials: One soft ball for students to toss to one another

Make the game more of a challenge by limiting the tenses or vocabulary that may be used. Set particular rules that students must follow. Some possibilities include not allowing use of the present tense, the words *and* or *the*, and the subject pronoun *I*. Set up fun consequences if students break the rule or have them sit out of the round and use that as a form of elimination.

Modification 2: Time's Up

Materials: Egg timer

Substitute an egg or other timer for the ball. Students pass it around the circle. When it goes off, the student with the timer stands up and says as much as possible of the sentence that was just formed. If the rendition was very good, you may offer some sort of prize.

Writing Extension 1

Materials: Blank sheet of paper

After completing the activity, ask students to write down as much of each sentence as they can. The person closest to the sentences that were formed can win a prize.

Writing Extension 2

Materials: Whiteboard, dry-erase marker, blank sheet of paper

Brainstorm a list of the most common and most interesting words that were used during the game. As a group, make up a few new sentences using that vocabulary. Then ask students to write their own sentences from the brainstorm. Give them a particular tense to focus on or just let them decide.

Label It in Time

Objectives: Match pictures or words to their pair in the target language.

Materials: Interactive whiteboard or magnetic whiteboard, magnet clips or adhesive magnet strips, vocabulary flashcards pictures, vocabulary word cards to match the pictures, timer

Activity Directions and Preparation Hints

This is a great way to make use of your vocabulary picture flashcards. You will need a magnetic whiteboard. Depending on the surface, you could attach a small piece of a magnet strip to the back of your picture card. Make a matching word card on an index card or cardstock. Attach a small magnet piece to the back of it as well. Place the pictures and cards on the board and invite a student up to participate. An alternative is to use an interactive whiteboard and its accompanying software to move the items. Even if you do have an interactive whiteboard, you can add variety by creating the magnetic version at times as well. Either using the clock or a kitchen timer, give the student a specified amount of time to match up all of the pictures and words. This can be played in teams or just as an individual review. Depending on the difficulty of the words and ability of the students, you may want to allow pairs to work together to label the items.

Applications and Modifications

Modification 1: Beat the Clock!

Materials: Same materials as in original version

If playing this as a class game, set up the rules to give points to the team that labels the objects fastest.

Modification 2: To Practice Grammar

Materials: Magnetic whiteboard, magnets or magnetic strips, word flashcards for grammar practice

Use this as a way to practice grammar by creating cards that have nouns, verbs, direct objects, and prepositions. Then create cards that match the category. Students must identify that *bird* is the noun, *runs* is the verb, and so forth.

Modification 3: For Content and Culture

Materials: Magnetic whiteboard, magnets or magnetic strips, word flashcards for content and culture practice

Have students practice content and culture through this method as well. Students can match dates and their importance, works of art and their creators, and so on. Get beyond the basic matching element by asking the students to write or discuss something about a few or all of the pairs on the board after they have been correctly matched.

Sample Topics:

- Fruits and vegetables
- Animals
- Furniture
- Plants and trees
- Household items
- Parts of the body
- The rainforest
- Weather

- Professions
- Clocks and times

Off to the Races!

Objectives: Recall information about any topic.

Materials: Laminated pictures, personal whiteboard, magnets

Activity Directions and Preparation Hints

This is a flexible game that allows you to review any material. Prepare a list of the questions you would like to review. You will need to find pictures of either horses or cars to use on the racetrack. Find one car or horse for each team. Look for different colored cars or number your horses to differentiate them from one another. Once the horses or cars are ready, draw a racetrack on the whiteboard. Divide students up into the number of teams you would like. Give each student a whiteboard. Ask the questions, and ask all students to write a response on their whiteboard. Students on each team must discuss their answers and decide on the best one. The team spokesperson shows the teacher the answer. If correct, the team moves their car or horse ahead one spot on the track. The first team to the finish line wins!

Oh No!

Objectives: Recall information about any topic.

Materials: Prepared list of questions, personal whiteboards, dry-erase markers

Activity Directions and Preparation Hints

This is a flexible game that allows you to engage all students and review any material you would like. It works well in a whole-class game situation as well as in smaller groups. If it is played in small groups, one student must act as the leader, who asks the questions and verifies the answers. To play this class game you need a list of vocabulary words, topics, questions, translations, and so forth that you want students to review. Each question should have a point value, generally beginning at 1 and going to 25. Use larger numbers if you would like to review them. In the list write the exclamation, *Oh no!* in your target language next to various numbers, instead of a question. To begin the game, each student needs a whiteboard and a dry-erase marker. Divide students into two to three teams. Begin the game by allowing one team to choose a number. That number is the question number and the point value for the question. State the question, and ask all students to write down what they think the answer is. All students should compare answers and decide on one. The spokesperson for the team gives the answer. Points are awarded if the answer is correct. If the answer is incorrect, another team has an opportunity to steal the point. This motivates all students to participate in answering questions even when it is not their team's turn. Steals are worth double the points. If a student has the misfortune of choosing a number that has *Oh no!* next to it, the team loses all the points they acquired up to that point. Continue the game until a period of time ends or until you reach a certain number of points.

Pass It Up!

Objectives: Review any topic selected by the teacher.

Materials: Sets of word cards or a whiteboard and dry-erase markers

Activity Directions and Preparation Hints

Prepare a series of statements or questions, leaving a blank for the word you want students to fill in. The blanks can be any type of word, but words that fit in a certain category, such as subject pronouns, possessive adjectives, verbs, and so forth, work particularly well. Make a set of cards that includes an answer for each of the questions. Divide students into teams by rows and pass out a set of cards to each team. Ask students to gather together at the back desk with the cards spread out in front of them. Read the statement or question students must answer. Once students determine an answer, either one student needs to run the card up to you at the front or students need to go back to their desks and pass the card up the row to the first student in the row, who stands up with the card. Give a point to each team with a correct answer and an extra point to the first team with the correct response. Continue with the next round. If you don't have time to prepare the set of cards, substitute a whiteboard for the cards and have the students write down the answer and pass it up the row. Provide students with a list of possibilities to choose from, or require that the group figure them out without assistance. Depending on how complicated the question is, read the questions orally or display them on a board or screen.

Sample Tasks:

- Definite or indefinite articles: Say the noun and students choose the correct article.

- Verb conjugations: Give students cards with the verb endings on cards and various verb stems. Students find the right stem and combine it with its correct ending.

- Possessive adjectives: Show the sentence with the English possessive adjective written down in the answer blank, but in parentheses. Students then look at the gender and number of the noun that follows to determine the correct answer in the target language.

- Review literary characters or events: Read a situation that describes a character, and ask the students to bring up the name of the correct character. Or conversely, read the name of a character, and ask students to choose any adjectives that describe the character.

- Question words: Give students a question and its answer but without the question word. They need to bring you the correct question word.

Pictionary

Objectives: Draw pictures of vocabulary so teammates can guess the word in the target language.

Materials: Large whiteboard or small personal whiteboards for the class, dry-erase markers

Activity Directions and Preparation Hints

This game works best for easily illustrated vocabulary words and concepts. Use it to review content and cultural topics as well. In this game, students are given a word to draw. Their teammates must guess the word in a predetermined period of time. Divide the class into two teams. A student from one team comes to the board and draws the word that you show on a flashcard or vocabulary list. That team has the time you allot for them to guess. If they are unsuccessful, you may allow the other team to guess to steal the point. This keeps the nondrawing team more focused. Have teams take turns drawing and guessing. Award one point per round.

Applications and Modifications

Modification 1: Stand up!

Materials: Same as original activity

When students are playing in a large group and ready to guess, ask them to stand up instead of raising their hands as soon as they know the word. Pick either the first student who pops up or anyone who is standing.

Modification 2: For Small Groups

Materials: One whiteboard for each group, one dry-erase marker for each group

Play this game in small groups of four to six students. This more directly involves the students and gives them a chance to draw and speak more often. Circulate around the room and monitor their progress. Students can use personal whiteboards or paper if no whiteboards are available. For vocabulary, allow students to choose words from their vocabulary list or any they know if it is an open review format. Another way to set up the game is to give students a set of cards or a list of words and make one person in the group the list master. The list master is in charge of managing the game and telling the team members what to draw.

Modification 3: Play in Rows

Materials: One whiteboard per row, one dry-erase marker per row

To play Pictionary by rows, you need one personal whiteboard per row. Paper can be substituted. The first person in the row comes to the front of the room and is told the word to draw. The student goes back to his or her desk, draws the word, and then passes the board through the row. Play where the last person is the one who has to guess or where anyone in the row that figures it out can write down his or her guess and run back to the front of the room to give the answer to you. Award points either to the first person who returns with the correct answer or to all teams with a correct answer. The game continues with students changing seats so either the last person in the row or the person who guessed the word comes to the front to be the next drawer. This version gets students moving and keeps them more involved.

Presents

Objectives: Brainstorm objects that could be given as gifts; use noun-adjective agreement when describing the gifts with an adjective; generate a list of likes and dislikes; choose an object for someone based on his or her likes and dislikes and explain why it is a good choice.

Materials: Object cards, statement cards

Activity Directions and Preparation Hints

This fun game reviews many verbs and categories of nouns. It is best used with action verbs and any nouns that can be given to someone. Use this format to practice other grammatical structures and verb tenses. Have students help brainstorm a list in the target language with all of the possible items from a vocabulary list that could be bought as a gift for someone. Have them add an adjective to the noun to practice description as well. Assign one word to each student and ask them to write it on the index card you give them. Now, have students brainstorm a list of preferences or likes. (He loves to swim. She likes the cold. He prefers chocolate ice cream.) Ask students to think of other students in the class while they brainstorm to try to guess things that person would like or would like to do. After you have a good list, assign one sentence to each student to write down on the index card. Collect them and divide the class into teams of four. Give each group four cards, each with a gift written on it. Select one of the statement cards and read it to the class—for example, "He loves to run!" Each group collaborates to see if they hold a gift card that would be appropriate to give to that person. Each group gives their best card to the scorekeeper. The scorekeeper reads the cards out loud and gives a point to the group who has an appropriate gift for the person described. An additional point can be earned if the students can identify a person in the class to which the statement applies. Redistribute the cards that were collected to new groups, and allow groups to exchange a card with another group if they wish. Play more rounds. Also play the game by asking students to find the gift that would be the least appropriate for the person's interests.

Applications and Modifications

Writing Extension

Materials: Object and statement cards, personal whiteboards, blank sheet of paper

Write various pairs of objects and statements on the board, and ask students to pick a number of pairs and write sentences about them. Vary the sentence structure based on the level you are teaching. A student could write something such as, "He needs new shoes because he likes to run." Another possibility would be to hand out one noun and one statement card to each pair and have them either make a connection between the two or say why they don't go together. Ask students to write more than one sentence by leaving their cards on their desks, standing up, and moving to a spot with more card pairs. With this type of activity you can also practice negative statements. If the student had a kite and likes to play outside, the statement could become, "He does not need a kite because he doesn't like to play outside." As a homework assignment, ask the students to write sentences about themselves using the pattern you practiced in class.

Sample Vocabulary Topics:

- Clothing

- Food

- Animals

- Items you might find on a rummage sale

- Electronic devices

- Things you use for a day at the beach

Sample Tasks:

- Likes and dislikes

- Things one loves or hates to do

- Things one prefers to or not to do

- Activities someone would or would not like to do in the future

- Activities someone did or did not do in the past

- What you would do if you won the lottery

Ring a Word

Objectives: Recall vocabulary words by matching the word in English with its counterpart in the target language; a context clue can also be substituted for the word in English to keep things in the target language.

Materials: Whiteboard with activity words written on it, dry-erase markers

Activity Directions and Preparation Hints

This game practices vocabulary recognition and can be used to review any vocabulary word. It can be applied to vocabulary, grammar, culture, or content. Write the words that you are teaching randomly on the board. Make sure to have two or more of each word. Divide the class into two teams. Give each team a different colored dry-erase marker or interactive whiteboard pen. When you call out the word in the students' native language, one person from each team runs to the board and circles the word in the target language. You can award points to both students who find it or give two points to the first one and one point to the second. The team with the most points wins.

Applications and Modifications

Application 1: Countries and Capitals

Materials: Whiteboard with activity words written on it, dry-erase markers or interactive whiteboard markers

Apply this to geography by listing the capitals of target language–speaking countries on the board. Call out the country and have the student circle the correct capital.

Modification 1: Pair Game

Materials: Sheet(s) of paper with the words from the activity on it

Make this game into a pair activity as well. Using the same or separate sheets, students race to see which partner can circle the correct answer first. List the words in a long column for each student. The order for the words could be the same or different. Listing the words in a column differentiates it a little more from the pair version of the flyswatter game.

Sample Topics:

- Sports, professions, school supplies, and so on (any vocabulary topic using the native and target languages)

- Synonyms

- Antonyms

- Cities and their famous landmarks

- Objects and how they are used (bowl to eat cereal out of, chair to sit on, etc.)

- Verb tenses and a verb that is written in that tense

- Countries and their currency

- Famous authors and their novels

Row Races

Objectives: Recall information about any topic.

Materials: One whiteboard for each row, one dry-erase marker for each row

Activity Directions and Preparation Hints

This game is effective for any topic you would like to review. It works particularly well for verbs and category-related grammar and vocabulary topics. Have students sit in a row of five to six people. Give the first person in the row a whiteboard and a marker. If you are practicing verb conjugation, give them a verb and the tense. Tell students to begin. The first students in line write the first-person singular form of the verb and pass the boards and markers to the students behind them. The second students write the second-person singular form and pass the boards and markers. The third students write the third-person singular form. Continue through the row, writing the plural forms of the verbs. The last student can run the board up to the front to have you check it, or you can have the students pass the board back up the row and ask the students to double-check for any errors. Award points for accuracy and speed. The first team with the correct answers gets five points, the second team gets four points, and so on. Another way to determine points is to let the students roll a die for points if their answer is correct.

Applications and Modifications

Use this game to review vocabulary, grammar, content, and cultural information. Verbs are easy to have students review without any setup time involved. Category topics work well, too. If food is the topic, one option is to ask each student to write a food vocabulary word. Make it more complicated by asking the students to write a question or statement using the food word in it. If you want students to work on topics that don't fit into a clear category, show students what each person in the row is responsible for, so there is no confusion. For example, if the topic is *A day at the beach* and you don't want just a list of nouns, try a format like this:

Student one writes: Something you eat at the beach

Student two writes: Something you always see at the beach

Student three writes: Something you do at the beach

Student four writes: With whom you go to the beach

Student five writes: When you go to the beach

Student six writes: Why you go to the beach

Sample Topics:

- Verb conjugations

- Possessive adjectives

- Pronouns

- Days of the week

- Famous buildings and their locations

- Things you keep in your room

- What you would find at a rummage sale

Scattergories

Objectives: Recall vocabulary from specific categories.

Materials: Letter cards, list of categories to review, sheet of paper divided into three columns

Activity Directions and Preparation Hints

This is a game that works well for reviewing categories of words. Provide students with a review of material you taught earlier in the year, in a current unit, or in previous level. With more advanced students, play this game in its traditional format. Have students form pairs. One partner competes against the other. Give students a sheet of paper divided into three columns with space for ten words in each column. Give students the name of a category, and pick a letter from a set of letter cards you make. Give the students about 90 seconds to write down as many words as they can think of that start with the letter for their category. After you call time, students should compare their words. Students get a point for each word they have on their paper that their partner does not. Students should keep track of their points for each round.

Applications and Modifications

Modification 1: For Beginning Students

Materials: Letter cards, list of categories to review, sheet of paper divided into three columns

Instead of asking students to find words in a category starting with one particular letter, allow them to write as many words from the category that start with any letter. Score the game as explained earlier. You may also want to let them play in pairs against another pair.

Modification 2: For Small Group Play

Materials: List of categories to review, sheet of paper divided into three columns or whiteboards and dry-erase markers

Allow students to play in small groups and work at their own pace. Give students a list of topics, and allow them to choose one for each round. Allow students to choose a letter for each category or to write down any word that fits the category. Students may use the sheet you give them with the three columns or a whiteboard. Ask to see their lists at the end of the period and/or monitor their progress by moving around the room and doing informal checks of their work.

Writing Extension

Materials: Blank sheet of paper, game sheets

After the game ask students to pick 10 of the words they have on their lists and work with their partner to write a poem, short story, paragraph, song, and so forth.

Scrabble

Objectives: Form words as a review of vocabulary.

Materials: Scrabble board (Figure 7.6)

Activity Directions and Preparation Hints

Students play this modification of the original Scrabble game in pairs or in two teams of no more than two players per team. Using the game board (see Figure 7.6), one student begins the game by writing down a word in the target language in the game squares. At least one letter of the word must touch the asterisk in the middle of the game board. The first student should try to write the longest word they know to give the game better possibilities for the words that follow. The first student then totals the points from the boxes that hold a letter of the word and writes down his or her points for the round. The game continues with the second player, who writes in a word. The word must connect in one place with the first player's original word. No player may write a word immediately next to another, unless logical words are formed at both the vertical and horizontal connection points. If the player succeeds in forming two words from one, he or she gets the points from both words. For this particular version of the game, if the number on the Scrabble board is written in bold, the value of the letter doubles; if it is underlined and in italics, the value of the entire word is tripled.

Simon Says

Objectives: Recall and act out vocabulary by responding to a leader's commands.

Materials: None

Activity Directions and Preparation Hints

Simon Says is a good way to get students to actively review vocabulary. A teacher or student stands in front of the classroom and is the leader or Simon. Simon tells students what to do, and students must follow the direction only if *Simon Says* is stated before the command. If students follow the directions and *Simon Says* is not stated, they must sit down and are out for the round. Simon can try to confuse participants by telling them to do one action while showing a different one.

My partner's points															
My points															

Scrabble board grid:

13	1	1	2	1	_3_	1	1	1	3	1	2	1	1	13
10	1	1	1	1	1	1	1	1	_1_	1	1	1	1	**10**
1	5	**3**	**1**	1	1	1	3	3	1	1	1	3	9	1
1	9	8	3	1	_1_	2	3	3	1	1	**3**	8	5	1
4	1	1	7	1	1	1	**2**	1	1	1	7	1	1	4
2	1	1	1	**6**	1	1	1	1	1	6	**1**	1	1	**2**
1	2	2	1	1	5	3	3	3	_5_	1	**1**	2	2	1
1	1	1	1	1	1	4	1	4	1	1	1	1	1	1
3	4	_5_	4	**3**	2	1	*	1	2	3	4	5	4	3
1	1	1	2	3	1	_4_	1	4	1	**3**	2	1	1	1
1	2	1	1	1	_5_	3	**3**	3	5	1	1	1	2	1
2	1	**2**	1	_6_	1	1	1	1	1	_6_	1	2	1	2
4	1	1	7	1	_1_	1	2	1	1	1	7	1	1	**4**
1	_3_	8	5	4	3	2	1	2	3	**4**	5	_8_	3	1
1	9	3	1	1	1	1	**3**	1	1	1	1	3	9	1
10	1	1	1	1	1	1	1	1	1	1	1	1	1	10
13	1	1	_2_	1	**3**	1	_1_	1	**3**	1	_2_	1	1	13

*Numbers that are in bold double the letter's value.
*Numbers that are in italics and underlined triple the word's value.

Figure 7.6 Scrabble Board

eRESOURCES

Applications and Modifications

Modification 1: Create Complex and Novel Directions

Materials: None

Make Simon Says trickier by giving multiple commands for students to do and comprehend—for example, "Touch your head with your right hand and jump while turning around." Add novelty to the actions by asking students to do strange things, such as, "Sit on the floor, raise your arms and legs and jump." Giving them commands that are bizarre and/or challenging adds interest and keeps them engaged.

Sample Topics:

- Classroom commands

- Airport directions

- Any action verbs

- Body parts

- Sports

- Weather expressions

- Household chores

Spud

Objectives: Recall and say the words from a vocabulary category.

Materials: One soft ball for students to toss to one another

Activity Directions and Preparation Hints

This game is an old childhood favorite that is fun to play with words in the target language. It works well with basic vocabulary after the students are comfortable saying it and can remember most or all of the words from a category you have taught. Play the game with famous people, countries, or capitals, as well as other basic content or cultural vocabulary. The game is best played outside or in an open area like a gym. Students form a circle around the student in the center. Give each student a number in the target language. The student in the center throws the ball up in the air, yells out a number, and runs away from the center. The student whose number was called runs to catch the ball. If the student catches the ball, the thrower gets the letter S. Meanwhile, the other students are running away from the center. As soon as the student whose number was called has possession of the ball, he or she yells, "Spud!" All students running must stop and stand motionless. The student with the ball can take up to three running steps toward any person. The goal is to hit a person with the ball. Stationary people may not move their feet but may duck or dodge the ball. If the stationary person catches the ball, the thrower gets the letter S. However, if hit, the student gets the letter S and is now in the center. The game continues. When students get all the letters S-P-U-D, they are out. Make sure to tell students that they may not aim at someone's head. If playing in Spanish, ALTO works well for the name of the game, because it means *stop*.

Sample Topics:

- Alphabet

- Numbers

- Animals

- Colors

- Names of famous people or literary figures

- Countries and/or capitals

- Household items

- Classroom objects

- Commands or action verbs (must do the command or action corresponding to the word before running away)

- Irregular conjugations in the past tense

Tic-Tac-Toe

Objectives: Recall and write vocabulary.

Materials: Whiteboards, dry-erase markers

Activity Directions and Preparation Hints

Play Tic-Tac-Toe to review any material and add a little competition. Pair students up and give each a whiteboard and a dry-erase marker. Ask students to determine who will be X and who will be O for the Tic-Tac-Toe game. They should draw a Tic-Tac-Toe board in the corner of one or both of their whiteboards. The student using X has the first opportunity to mark on the Tic-Tac-Toe board. Begin the game by asking the students a question to which they all must respond on their whiteboards. Even though it is X's chance to win a spot on the Tic-Tac-Toe board, O must also write; if X gets the answer wrong, O has a chance to steal the turn and put an O on the board. Students should show you their boards so you can visually check the answers and verify if they are correct. A second option is to have a list of the answers prepared for the students so they can self-check. If the X student is correct, X puts an X on the board and the next round is for O to win a spot on the board. If O steals the round because X gives an incorrect answer, O has the chance to mark an O on the board two rounds in a row.

Applications and Modifications

Modification 1: Large-Group Play

Materials: Projected Tic-Tac-Toe grid

Play this game as a class as well. Make and project a Tic-Tac-Toe Grid to use as the class board. All students should still write the answers, and one student will raise his or her hand to give an answer for the team. Use all of the rules from the preceding explanation for group play as well.

Modification 2: Pair Play

Materials: Tic-Tac-Toe board

On a Tic-Tac-Toe board template, type or write in one question, statement, vocabulary word, or translation you would like the students to practice in each spot of board. For students to win the spot, they must provide a correct answer to the question in it. Give students an answer sheet, or allow them to look up answers on a vocabulary sheet. Another option is to have a third person in the group be in charge of verifying answers with the master answer sheet.

There's No Subject

Objectives: Select an appropriate subject for a sentence where it is left out.

Materials: Sentence strips with the subject omitted or a list of sentences with omitted subjects on an interactive whiteboard or projected on a screen

Activity Directions and Preparation Hints

Write various target language sentences leaving out the subject—for example, "My_____ is the son of my grandparents. _____ is what I use to dry my hair." Cut the sentences into strips and put them into a hat. The big sombreros are nice for Spanish class. Divide the class into two teams. Teams alternate choosing a sentence from the hat and filling in the missing word. Award one point per correct answer. You can also write the sentences using interactive whiteboard software and uncover the questions one by one if you do not want to cut out strips. Allow students to offer an oral response or ask them to write the response on a whiteboard.

Sample Topics:

- Personal hygiene items
- Professions
- Pets
- Furniture and other household items
- Famous people
- Students in the classroom or well-known school staff
- Food
- Places in the city
- Things you do and find in an airport
- Hotel items

Verb War

Objectives: Students conjugate verbs.

Materials: One set of pronoun cards per group, one set of infinitive cards per group

Activity Directions and Preparation Hints

You need one set of pronoun and one of infinitive cards per group for this verb conjugation game. If possible, color-code the sets of cards. To make the cards, use the table feature in a word processing document. Type the pronoun cards into one table and the infinitives into another. Copy the pronoun master onto one color of cardstock and the infinitives onto another. Save time by having the students cut the cards out before playing. Reuse the cards to practice conjugations in various tenses. Once the cards are cut out, the students are ready to play. Tell students what verb tense they should play with. One student turns over a card from the pronoun deck while the other turns over the card in the infinitive deck. The first student to correctly conjugate the verb wins the round. Students should play various rounds.

Applications and Modifications

Modification 1: Single Pronoun Play

Materials: One set of pronoun cards per group, one set of infinitive cards per group

One modification of this game is to have students use the same pronoun card and use different infinitives. This might be a good modification if the conjugation is new or more complicated. If students are beginning to practice a set of verbs with mixed endings (-*ar*, -*er*, -*ir* in Spanish), it might also be helpful for students keep the same pronoun and focus on which ending they need to choose.

Writing Extension

Materials: One set of pronoun cards per group, one set of infinitive cards per group, blank sheet of paper

Ask students to pick 10 subjects and 10 infinitives cards. The students should use the two cards to write that number of statements or questions. Another possibility is to have them choose various infinitives and one or two subjects. Ask them to incorporate them into a story, dialogue, song, or other writing creation.

Sample Topics:

- Present-tense regular verbs
- Reflexive verbs
- Irregular verbs in the past tense
- Negative commands
- Present perfect

Vocabulary Puzzles

Objectives: Recall vocabulary and match the English word with its target language equivalent by doing a puzzle.

Materials: Vocabulary puzzle (Figure 7.7)

Activity Directions and Preparation Hints

The vocabulary puzzle is a versatile tool to review vocabulary, grammar, culture, and content-based topics. Using the vocabulary puzzle template (see Figure 7.7), write a word in the target language on one piece and its equivalent in English on a matching piece. You can choose to leave the puzzle border without words or add in extras to make the puzzle more complicated. Repeating words within the puzzle will also create more of a challenge. Save time by having the students cut out the puzzle pieces before starting the activity. Make copies of the puzzle on different colors to reduce the confusion of what piece goes with which puzzle if they are separated. If you plan to use the puzzle a lot, consider copying it onto cardstock. Coin-sized envelopes work nicely for storing the pieces if they are not too large. Store all the little envelopes in a sandwich bag, and label the bag with a permanent marker.

Applications and Modifications

Vocabulary puzzles can be used to review any grammar, culture, content-based, or general unit vocabulary. The only limitation is the size of the puzzle piece, which will determine how long of a word or phrase can be used.

Writing Extensions

Materials: Vocabulary puzzle (Figure 7.7), blank sheet of paper

Extend this activity by asking students to write sentences using the vocabulary found in the puzzle. Challenge them to write the longest, logical sentence they can, using as much of the vocabulary in the puzzle as possible.

Sample Topics:

- Artists and musicians and their art style or work

- Historical figures and their contribution

- Capitals and their countries

- Presidents and their countries

- Literary works and their characters

- Singers and songs

- Vocabulary in English and the target language

- Synonyms

- Antonyms

- Numbers

- Item descriptions and the item

- Questions and answers

- A subject/infinitive and the correct conjugation (I/to drink—I drink)

Other Uses

- Use the vocabulary to write a letter to someone.

- Write a dialogue to present to the class.

- Write a song.

the only child — your nephew	tu sobrino — his dad — mi madrastra	su papá — our niece — nuestra casa	nuestra sobrina — his cousins
el hijo único — his mom — su tío	my stepmother — su mamá — tu padre — his son	our house — your father — su hijo — their stepfather	sus primos — su padrastro — their son
their uncle — tu hermana — mi familia	su hijo — your sister — tu tía — su abuelo	their child — your aunt — her grandson — our sisters	su hijo — su nieto — my brother
my family — nuestro primo — her daughter	their grandpa — our cousin — mis parientes — mis padres	nuestras hermanas — my relatives — their dog — su gato	mi hermano — su perro — nuestros hijos
su hija — su abuela	my parents — his grandma — mi primo	her cat — my cousin — our grandparents	our children — nuestros abuelos

Figure 7.7 Vocabulary Puzzle Template

- Create a drawing that incorporates words from the puzzle. Students can then label the words.

- For a puzzle based on a novel, ask students to choose one of the characters of a literary work, discuss that person in more detail, and create a portrait of what they think that person looks like.

What Do You Remember?

Objectives: Recall topics to answer review questions.

Materials: Two different lists of questions and answers

Activity Directions and Preparation Hints

Use this game as a way to review any vocabulary, grammar, content, or cultural topic. Play it as a whole-class game if you would like to monitor all of the answers given more closely. Allow the game to be played in small groups if you would like more students to have the opportunity to participate. Prepare by creating two lists of things you would like your students to practice. Each list should have the question, vocabulary word, or sentence to be translated in the left column and the answer in the right. Make the questions harder as the list continues, and assign point values to each question. The easiest way to assign the point values is by numbering the questions in order, and the number preceding the question is its value. The lists should have few if any questions that are repeated between the two lists, because this quiz game is played by two opposing teams. Give members of each team a whiteboard so they can compose their answers. Provide each team one list of questions and answers. The teams begin play by taking turns asking each other to answer the questions on their lists in writing or orally. They can ask any question on their list at any time. Students get the point value for the question they answer. Determine a number of rounds they will play or create a time limit.

Sample Topics:

- Identify professions.

- Identify important contributions of famous people in Latin America.

- Translate sentences found on common household product labels.

- Conjugate irregular verbs and put them in a sentence.

- Give a synonym or antonym for the stated word.

- Answer questions about your daily routine.

What's in the Bag?

Objectives: Form questions to guess what an object is after feeling it in a bag.

Materials: Bag, objects to put in a bag

Activity Directions and Preparation Hints

For this game, create a bag of objects. Students must not be able to see into the bag. Students take turns putting their hands in the bag and trying to identify the object they touched. The students try to guess the object and ask the teacher in the target language, "Is it a . . . ?" If they are correct, they can take it out of the bag and get a point for their team. As a follow-up to the game, ask students to write sentences, a brief paragraph, or a story about the objects from the bag. You may want to display them on the table as a reminder of what was in the bag.

Applications and Modifications

Modification 1: What Is It?

Materials: Bag, objects for the bag

Put one item in a bag that students cannot see. Allow them to ask questions about it to try to figure out what it is. The person who guesses what the object is can get a point for his or her team, have the object, or win a different prize. Play the game once or with various rounds, changing the object each time.

Word Race Game

Objectives: Form words from random letter combinations.

Materials: List of letter combinations

Activity Directions and Preparation Hints

Review any vocabulary students have learned with this game. Prepare a list of various combinations of letters before the game or determine them on the spot. Divide students into groups of four, and give them paper or white-boards and dry-erase markers. Write the random letter combinations on the board for that round. Ask students to make as many words as they can, using only those letters. One person should record the words for each group. Ask the spokesperson from each team to read the words on their list. The other teams must listen and cross out any words they have in common. Have the teams bring their lists to the front, and award each team a point for each word on their list that is not crossed off.

Applications and Modifications

Writing Extension

Materials: Word lists from the game, blank sheet of paper

Once the game is completed, direct the groups to select 10 words from their lists. Ask them to pair up and do one of the following:

- Write a sentence that uses all of the words.

- Form various logical or illogical sentences.

- Create questions using those words.

- Invent a short story.

Five-Minute Activities to Stretch Your Legs and Brain

Activity & Brief Description	Page	Application Areas				Type of Communication	
		VO	GR	CO	CU	Oral	Written
Alphabetized Adjectives Students state short sentences where the next adjective always starts with the next letter of the alphabet. You may also put requirements on the first letter of the subject—in this case, C: *Camila is antsy; Caroline is beautiful.*	163	•	•			•	•
Answering Questions With Questions* Students must ask a question to remain in the round. The following student does not answer the question, but instead forms another question.	163	•	•			•	•
Can You Come to the Party?* Begin by making this statement (or a similar one based on the grammatical function you want to practice): "I am going to the party and I am bringing ___." Students must figure out what type of item fits in your category. Then students make the same statement and fill with that item. If they don't guess something that fits in the category, they cannot *go to the party* and are eliminated from that round.	164	•	•			•	•
Categorize It!* Pick a category for review. Students must state an item from that category to stay in the game. If they repeat a word already stated or can't say a word, they are out and must sit down.	164	•				•	
Five-Letter Words* Students must state a five-letter word (two-letter, three-letter, and so on) to remain in the competition. Make it more of a challenge by limiting the words to specific topics.	165	•				•	•
Grammatically Correct Nonsense Sentences* Students take turns adding words to form a sentence that is grammatically correct but nonsensical. If a student adds something that is not grammatically correct, or cannot add a word, they are out and must sit down.	165	•	•			•	

Activity & Brief Description	Page	Application Areas				Type of Communication	
		VO	GR	CO	CU	Oral	Written
Guess That Noun! One student leaves the room while the rest of the class decides on the word that student must guess. The returning student can ask three questions: (1) Why do you like this thing? (2) When do you like this thing? (3) Where do you like this thing? The student can call on any audience member to answer one of the three questions. The student must give as much information possible in the answer to help the person guessing figure it out.	166	•	•			•	
Say It!* A student states a word from any category. The next student must say a word that starts with the last letter of the previous student's word. Change it up and ask the students to use the second letter or the same first letter or the previous word.	167	•				•	•
Tricky Sentences* Challenge students to keep a sentence going for as long as possible where each word starts with the same letter. Allow the sentence to be silly as long as it is grammatically correct. Students sit down if they can't think of a word or if it is incorrect. New sentences can be started with a different letter only after a sentence has been completed: *Sara Sandra Smith saw Sam Stewart Swanson swimming silently while softly singing serenades*.	167	•	•			•	•
Word Associations Begin the game by saying any word in Spanish that your students are familiar with, or let a student begin. The next student provides a word that is somehow associated with the first word. If they cannot, or nobody understands the connection they made, they must sit down. Continue until there is only one student left.	169	•	•			•	•

*All activities in this section with an asterisk are played orally with students standing up and in an elimination-style format. Once an incorrect answer is given, that student must sit down. Most can also be used as written activities.

VO = Vocabulary   GR = Grammar   CO = Content   CU = Culture

Alphabetized Adjectives

Objectives: Recall adjectives and form descriptive sentences.

Materials: None

Activity Directions and Preparation Hints

Students orally state sentences where the subject always starts with the same letter, but the adjective changes alphabetically, starting with A. Ask students to change the subject each time, or allow them to repeat subjects. Vary the activity by having students alphabetize the subject and adjective.

Example Sequence

Camila is able.

Carmen is beautiful.

Carlos is careful.

Carolina is diligent.

Carmela is friendly.

Answering Questions With Questions

Objectives: Practice question formation.

Materials: None

Activity Directions and Preparation Hints

Students must ask a question to stay in the game. Instead of answering the question that the previous student asked, they have to ask another question. Because this is a challenge, students must form grammatically correct questions or they are out.

Example Sequence

Student 1 asks: What is your favorite color?

Student 2 asks: What did you do last night?

Student 3 asks: Did Sofia dance with Pedro on Friday?

Student 4 asks: Where is Carmen?

Student 5 asks: Why doesn't he do his homework?

Applications and Modifications

Make the activity more of a challenge by limiting the students to a particular verb tense. Also, consider determining a minimum word requirement for each question.

Can You Come to the Party?

Objectives: Practice the formation of statements in a variety of tenses.

Materials: None

Activity Directions and Preparation Hints

Decide the type of statement formation you want students to practice. The basic structure is: *I am going to a party and I am taking a _____*. Pick a category of items from which the student must take something to be able to go to the party, but do not tell the students what it is. You begin the round by stating an example so the students can try to figure out the pattern. If they don't say something that fits the pattern, they can't go to the party and have to sit down. Begin the game by making a statement with a word that fits in the category. The goal is to be the last student standing who can also state what the pattern was.

Example Sequence

Teacher begins with:	I am going to the party and I am taking raspberries.
Student 1 states:	I am going to the party and I am taking apples.
Teacher responds:	Yes, you are going to the party.
Student 2 states:	I am going to the party and I am taking a kiwi.
Teacher responds:	No, you aren't going.
Student 3 states:	I am going to the party and I am taking strawberries.
Teacher responds:	Yes, you are going.

(In this case students needed to state a red fruit to be able to go to the party.)

Applications and Modifications

This is a fun way to practice a grammatical structure that you want students to hear and say multiple times. Change the structure of the statement to reinforce a structure you are teaching. Have the students ask a question about whether they can go as well. See the following sample question modifications:

I would like to come to your party and bring you a _____. Can I come?

I want to go to the party at your house. Can I bring you _____?

I went to my friend's party. I took _____. Did they let me in?

I hope to go to your party if you let me. I want to bring _____. Will you let me in?

I would go to your anniversary party if I could bring _____.

I will go to your birthday party and I will bring _____. Is that okay?

Categorize It!

Objectives: Recall vocabulary from a chosen category.

Materials: None

Activity Directions and Preparation Hints

Begin by picking a category. To stay in the game, students must provide a word that fits in the category. If they can't, they must sit down.

Sample Topics:

- Fruits

- Foods

- Sports and leisure activities

- Action verbs

- Words associated with Christmas

- Thanksgiving

- Clothing items and related words

- The rainforest

Five-Letter Words

Objectives: Activate previous knowledge of vocabulary to think of words with a specific number of letters.

Materials: None; modified activities may require additional materials.

Activity Directions and Preparation Hints

Students must say a five-letter word to stay in the round. Depending on their language level, let students to do a quick brainstorm alone or with their partner. Allow them to write down their words. Once again, depending on their level, you may want to let them use their sheets the first time you do this activity. If not, ask them to either recycle the sheet or put it away. Students are out when they cannot say a five-letter word. Play again by changing the number of letters in the word.

Applications and Modifications

Writing Application

Materials: Blank sheet of paper

This is also easily adapted into a written activity. Ask students to write as many five-letter words as they can in the period of time you give them. They can play against a partner, in a small group, or against the whole class. Students earn a point for each word that their partner does not have on their list.

Grammatically Correct Nonsense Sentences

Objectives: Practice grammar in a humorous context.

Materials: None; modified activities may require additional materials.

Activity Directions and Preparation Hints

This type of activity encourages your students to look at words in a more creative way. To play, students work together to form sentences that are grammatically correct but make no sense. Each student may say only one word. The first student begins with the subject, and then students continue to add words going around the room in order. Students who cannot provide a word that fits in the sentence so that it is grammatically correct must sit down. Limit the students to a specific tense or sentence structure to create more of a challenge. Allow any length of sentence, or determine a specific requirement for the number of words in it.

Examples

- The gigantic dog drives to the zoo to take pictures of the little elephants.

- The sad book went to the library to check out a funny person.

- The glass of sour milk hopped on the tired table.

- The blanket went to find a big cat to keep it warm.

- The purple apple is generous and gives its green couch to the sad onion.

Applications and Modifications

Application 1: Noun-Adjective Agreement

Materials: Blank sheet of paper

Focus on descriptive sentences, and require students to have at least one adjective in every sentence. Reinforce the noun-adjective order and agreement that students tend to struggle with in languages where the order is reversed as compared to English. If the order is wrong or the adjective does not agree with the noun in gender and number, the student has to sit down. This causes students to think more about applying the rules correctly. Depending on the students' level and adjective base, ask students to focus on particular types of adjectives: feelings, physical or personality traits, or size.

Guess That Noun!

Objectives: Guess a noun from three clues.

Materials: None

Activity Directions and Preparation Hints

A student must guess a noun after asking three questions about it. One student volunteers or is designated as the person to guess the noun. Send that student into the hallway while the class decides the noun to use for the activity, or have a list of nouns and tell the students which word to use. Call the student in the hallway back into the classroom. That student may ask only three questions. The students answering the questions must give as complete of an answer to the question as possible.

Example: The Ice Cream

- Why do you like it?   I like it because it is cold and sweet.
- When do you like it?   I like it on a hot summer day.
- Where do you like it?   I like to eat it at the Dairy Queen.

Applications and Modifications

Modification: Are They Lying?

Materials: None

Throw an additional twist into the activity by allowing the students who respond to the questions about the object to lie. If the questioning student suspects that they are lying, they can ask another student to corroborate answers. The second student may not lie.

Say It!

Objectives: Activate prior vocabulary to practice a variety of words.

Materials: None; modified activities may require additional materials.

Activity Directions and Preparation Hints

A student says a word from any category to start (Figure 8.1). The next student must say a word that starts with the last letter of the previous student's word. Also try the activity using the same first or second letter instead.

Applications and Modifications

Writing Extension

Materials: Blank sheet of paper

Have a couple of students keep a list of words that were used, or ask students to try to remember the ones they used. Write up a list on the board, and ask students to write silly sentences, a set of questions, a story, or a poem with the vocabulary that was generated.

Tricky Sentences

Objectives: Practice sentence formation.

Materials: Blank sheet of paper

Activity Directions and Preparation Hints

In this challenging activity, students must go around the classroom and make sentences in which each word starts with the same letter. Allow the use of connection words, such as *in*, *on*, *to*, and the like to aid in sentence flow. Let the class pick the letter they want to use; or for more of a challenge, pick the letter yourself. New sentences can

Student	Last Letter	First Letter	Second Letter
1	paper	green	sizzle
2	ruler	gopher	igloo
3	real	grapefruit	glossy
4	leap	give	loop
5	perfume	ghost	overalls
6	elephant	gigantic	very

Figure 8.1 Category Examples

be started with a different letter only after a sentence has been completed. Students who cannot think of a word that fits or who state a word that is grammatically incorrect must sit down. Consider doing this as a written activity the first time so students can become comfortable with it.

Examples

- Caroline cautiously crossed Crosby's Crossing, careful not to crush crazy creeping crabs.

- Sara Sandra Smith saw Sam Stewart Swanson swimming silently while softly singing serenades.

Modification 1: Every Word Starts with the Following Letter of the Alphabet

Materials: Blank sheet of paper

Challenge students to create sentences where each word that follows starts with the next letter of the alphabet. Allow students to end sentences and continue with a new one starting with the next letter of the alphabet. Require that the sentences follow one another logically, or allow the sentences to contain unrelated ideas. Give students the freedom to choose connecting words that may not fit perfectly into the pattern. Do this as an oral or written activity.

Example

Ashley brings cakes during Fred's gathering housed in Josh King's luminous mansion.

Word Associations

Objectives: Activate background vocabulary knowledge to make associations between words.

Materials: Blank sheet of paper

Activity Directions and Preparation Hints

Begin by saying a word. Students must say something that they associate with that word. If the association makes sense, or they can explain quickly why it does in the target language, they stay in the round. Students who can no longer make an association sit down and are out. Let the associations roam free, or limit them to a particular category if you need to put more boundaries on the activity. Continue the game until there is only one student left. For an added bit of fun, have the student continue the round, going back and forth with you as many times as he or she can. This game can work well as an individual, pair, or small-group writing activity as well.

Example

- Student 1 says: hat

- Student 2 says: head

- Student 3 says: hair

- Student 4 says: razor

- Student 5 says: shaving cream

- Student 6 says: face

Resources and Bibliography

World Language Websites

#LangChat Blog: The #LangChat conversations on Twitter are summed up on the Calico Spanish blog link here. You can search the archives for topics of interest. It is a helpful way to stay on top of current topics.

http://blog.calicospanish.com

CARLA: The Center for Advanced Research on Language Acquisition (CARLA) has great resources for world language instruction and assessment.

www.carla.umn.edu

CLEAR: The Center for Language Education and Research offers free technology downloads that allow you to record and answer prompts, record and store videos online, and more!

http://clear.msu.ed/clear

Conjuguemos: Web site to practice verb conjugations and vocabulary; teachers can type in their own lists or use the ones already on the site.

www.conjuguemos.com

Duolingo: A self-paced language learning program available in many languages.

www.duolingo.com

Flickr (Creative Commons): Search Flickr photos under creative commons to more easily access pictures and know what rights you have to using them.

www.flickr.com/creativecommons

Freetech4teachers: This blog focuses on educational technology use and is an excellent resource.

www.freetech4teachers.com

Kahoot: This is an interactive, exciting response game that kids love.

https://getkahoot.com

Lingro: This site allows you to read in another language and be able to click on any word to have it defined as you read, as well as add the word to a word list to practice later.

http://lingro.com

Memrise: This site allows you to build an interactive course for vocabulary learning or find existing courses.

www.memrise.com

MYLO: This site has modules for learning simple to more complex topics in a variety of languages.

www.hellomylo.com

National Foreign Language Resource Centers: This site has links to all of the resource centers.

www.nflrc.org

Padlet: This site allows you to post sticky notes for organizing thoughts and pictures individually and/or collaboratively.

www.padlet.comc

Textivate: This site creates a variety of activities for students to do online or on paper (fee-based).

www.textivate.com

Twitter: You can use this microblogging site to connect and share with other educators and to keep current on other topics of interest. Follow your state and regional organizations. You may also want to follow: #actfl, #langchat, #edchat, #fliplang, #sk12, and #mlearning.

www.twitter.com

Quia: This site enables you to practice vocabulary and grammar through games (fee-based).

www.quia.com

Resources and Bibliography

Quizlet: This site creates flashcards and other games for class and student use (free and paid account options).
www.quizlet.com

Ultimate Camp Resource: This site has many icebreakers and other activities that can be adapted for use in the classroom.
www.ultimatecampresource.com

Wordreference: This online dictionary has a forum where you can get answers to questions you might have about grammar usage and vocabulary.
www.wordreference.com

Zondle: This site will create interactive games students can play using the questions that you upload or input.
www.zondle.com

172

Bibliography

Books

Blaz, Debora. (1999). *Foreign language teacher's guide to active learning.* Larchmont, NY: Eye On Education.

Blaz, Debora. (2001). *A collection of performance tasks and rubrics: Foreign languages.* Larchmont, NY: Eye On Education.

Bowman, Sharon. (2003). *How to give it so they get it: A flight plan for teaching anyone anything and making it stick.* Glenbrook, NY: Bowperson.

Fenton, Sue. (2003). *Power talk: Strategies and activities for speaking: 100s of ideas and cues.* Newington, CT: Madame Fifi.

Fenton, Sue. (2004). *You played a song. Now what? A survival guide for using songs in the classroom.* Newington, CT: Madame Fifi.

Meier, Dave. (2000). *The accelerated learning handbook: A creative guide to designing and delivering faster, more effective training programs.* New York: McGraw Hill.

Ojeda, Diego F. (2007). *Enhancing Spanish language instruction: Practical activities to strengthen your student's proficiency in Spanish.* Medina, WA: Institute for Educational Development.

Silberman, Mel. (1996). *Active learning: 101 strategies to teach any subject.* Boston: Allyn and Bacon.

Professional Conference Presentation

Gutschow, Erin, & Wagner, Gina. (2006, November). *A potpourri of possibilities . . . The mommy edition.* Paper presented at the World in Wisconsin, Wisconsin in the World: Proceedings of the Wisconsin Association of Foreign Languages, Appleton.

Internet

National Capital Language Resource Center: www.nclrc.org/essentials/index.htm

American Council on the Teaching of Foreign Languages proficiency guidelines: www.actfl.org

Center for Advanced Research on Language Acquisition Assessment Resources: www.carla.umn.edu/assessment/VAC/resources/index.html

Rubrics from Arlington County Schools: www.cal.org/twi/rubrics/oral1–5.pdf

Rubrics from Fairfax County Schools: www.fcps.k12.va.us/DIS/OHSICS/forlang/PALS/rubrics/index.htm

New Jersey World Languages Curriculum Framework: www.state.nj.us/njded/frameworks/worldlanguages/appendb.pdf#search=%22PALS%20assessments%20%2Bspanish%22

The Ultimate Camp Resource site: www.ultimatecampresource.com

Wisconsin's Model Academic Standards for Foreign Languages: http://dpi.state.wi.us/standards/pdf/fl.pdf

English as a Second Language Games: www.eslkidstuff.com/gamesmenu.htm